Time to Manage

An agenda for effective leadership

5WH

Robertson Hunter Stewart

This book is dedicated to

My wife Valerie,

My greatest supporter.

The author reserves the moral right to be identified as the author of this work.

The author of this work is:

Robertson Hunter Stewart
Born 1962, St Andrews, Scotland

Other books from the same author:

The Incredible Value of Employee Power Unleashed:
How to gain competitive advantage by treating your
employees well!
ISBN: 9781076872159 – June 2019 available on:

Amazon

USA: https://lnkd.in/dHty7XE
UK: https://lnkd.in/dxGq9QH

One to One

Managing   quality   time   with   individuals   for
engagement and success

ISBN: 979-8697224250 – October 2020 available on:

Amazon

USA: https://www.amazon.com/dp/B08L19V12Y

UK : https://www.amazon.co.uk/dp/B08L19V12Y

All titles also available on Apple and Kobo/FNAC

Website:

www.robertsonhunterstewart.com

Follow the author on:
Robertson Hunter Stewart @:

FOREWORD

Since our beginnings, we humans have been fascinated with the passing of time itself. However, on the global scale of things, our attempts to measure time have been relatively recent, dating back only as far as 5,000 to 6,000 years ago among ancient African and Middle Eastern (also known as Sumerian) cultures.

A lot of the information from that time has been either mislaid or lost entirely. On the other hand, some of the best-known and well-kept historical evidence of time measurement techniques and devices comes from ancient Egypt and Babylonia. The relationship to time for these later cultures was most often concerned with the seasons themselves to ensure that food crops were planted and harvested at the correct times to produce the best yields possible, nourishing their respective populations and avoiding famine at all costs. In actual fact, we could make a good case for ancient arable farming being the forerunner of calendars and agendas.

To find some of the first devices to measure time, we need to go back to ancient Egypt (circa 3500 BCE) where obelisks were used for this purpose. Basically, an obelisk is a four-sided column from which the shadow splits the day into morning and afternoon. It was also possible to tell the longest and shortest days of the year due to the length of the shadow itself at "noon".

Next came another Egyptian invention known as a sundial. Again using shadow, this could divide the sunlit part of the day into 10 different segments, along with what we would call the twilight hours in the morning and the evening.

Between ancient Egypt and the Middle Ages, a multitude of different objects and ways were used to measure and split time into increments. Examples include the hourglass, graduated candles and water clocks. It might come as something of a surprise to learn that pocket sundials based on ancient Egyptian principles were still all the rage well into the 10th century in England.

The next major advances in timekeeping came as late as the 14th century with the appearance of large mechanical clocks in Italy. Following on from that, innovation manifested in the form of the first spring-loaded clock, invented by Peter Henlein between 1500 and 1510, but we had to wait until the middle of the 19th century to see the "birth" of the modern wristwatch. There have been several different claims as to who made the first watch of this kind, but one of the most notable and interesting stories dates from the beginning of the 20th century.

In 1901, the Brazilian aviator and inventor Alberto Santos-Dumont complained to his friend Louis Cartier that it was extremely difficult to take out a pocket watch while flying as this action did not allow him to keep both hands on the wheel. Three years later in 1904, Cartier produced his first wristwatch. As a matter of interest, the luxury brand offers a line of watches named after Santos to this day.

Once we humans had a way to measure time with some accuracy, when did we actually start to manage it? The roots of time management are set in the 19th century with the advent of factories and the division of labour for mass producing goods. Factory work, unlike agricultural work, led to the introduction of shifts, meaning that people not only worked in daylight but also nocturnal hours, as factories ran on a 24-hour basis to maximise production. As a result, there was more need for punctuality and the accurate measurement of shift times.

Towards the end of the Industrial Revolution (between 1850 and 1914), Frederick Winslow Taylor came up with his theory of scientific management.[1] In this theory, Taylor summed up his techniques, the main objective being to improve the economic efficiency of industrial processes. In particular, Taylor believed that productivity, especially labour productivity, could be maximised through the use of scientific "instruments" such as time and motion studies. In other words, each part of a man or woman's job could be measured in terms of how they were carrying it out and in what amount of time.

This obviously went hand in hand with the division of labour, as people were becoming more and more specialised in one part of production rather than the overall process and creation of the finished goods. An example of Taylor's theory came with the first mass-produced car: the model T (1908) from the Ford Motor company. Each car moved along an assembly line, with the workers adding their own piece to create the whole, rather than being individually hand crafted. This process maximised production so much that automobiles became affordable to the general public for the first time.

Taylor's work on scientific management, often known as Taylorism, has been summarised as "a fair day's work for a fair day's pay". Although this is an oversimplification, it does hold true to a certain extent, as even today many company and organisation leaders are obsessed with the concept of productivity being the only source of efficiency, success and overall competitive advantage. We could say that Frederick Winslow Taylor was the father of time management.

There are several flaws in the paradigms associated with scientific management, the main one being that the performance of humans cannot be taken as a known constant in the same way as the speed of a machine part or the given weight of a raw material. It is impossible for a human being to produce at the same speed and efficiency throughout his or her life; we are not machines. Variables come about dependent on age, experience, motivation, health and environment. Something as simple as the temperature or lighting in the workplace can affect a person's efficiency, so a toxic environment with people setting out to hurt one another on a psychological level (for example, workplace bullying, micromanaging or moral harassment) is clearly going to be detrimental.

The Hawthorne Studies,[23] conducted by Elton Mayo and Fritz Roethlisberger at one of Western Electric Company's production plants in the 1920s, started out by recording the effect on productivity of altering physical conditions in the workplace. In the first phase of the experiment, alterations were made to the level of lighting and the results seemed to indicate that there was indeed a correlation between physical working conditions and productivity. However, in later parts of the study, Mayo and Roethlisberger observed that socio-psychological criteria also had an impact on work behaviours and productivity.

In 1958, while studying the results of the original Hawthorne report, Henry Landsberger came to the conclusion that the employees had performed better during the study simply because they had been singled out for *special attention* and it was this attention that had impacted the results more than any of the other criteria. He called this the **Hawthorne effect**.[4] As proof of this, work records at the time showed that productivity slumped badly when the Hawthorne Studies ended.

As you can see, we have two main schools of thought in discussions and debates on leadership and management today: Taylorism, with its emphasis on the efficiency of the process and the need for incentives for workers to produce their best, and the behavioural studies which indicate that extrinsic motivation is connected to socio-psychological criteria. As is often the case, the optimum solution cannot be found in the black and white of either school of thought. It's far more likely to reside in the "grey areas" between the two.

In this book, we will use both approaches to find the most effective agenda for leadership and efficient tools to manage it.

Effective leadership and efficient management practices need to be aligned if we wish to use the time we have at our disposal to our maximum advantage.

[1] Taylor, FW (1911) *The Principles of Scientific Management* (Harper & Brothers)

[2] Hart, CWM (1943) "The Hawthorne Experiments" (*The Canadian Journal of Economics and Political Science*, 9, 2, p.150)

[3] Gale, EAM (2004) "The Hawthorne Studies – A fable for our time?" (*QJM: An International Journal of Medicine* 97, 7, pp.439–449)

[4] Landsberger, HA (1958) *"Hawthorne Revisited"* (Ithaca, NY Cornell University)

TABLE OF CONTENTS

INTRODUCTION

Time to Manage

An agenda for effective leadership

5WH

INTRODUCTION

In both our work and personal lives, we all sooner or later have to come to grips with the fact that we only have a certain amount of time at our disposal. Time is a rare commodity and as we all know, anything rare can command a high price. Hence the expression "time is money".

Quite apart from its monetary value, the fact that time is a rare commodity means that we should treasure it and use it wisely. Once we've used our precious seconds, minutes or hours, we can't get them back again. Time is, therefore, a *highly perishable commodity.*

As more and more demands are made on our time, its value will increase due to its increasing rarity. There is always a cost attached to giving our time to a request from someone else or even a demand from ourselves, however good the reason for the demand may be, so I advise you to remember this: as a leader or a manager, we don't always have to acquiesce. Just because we see our time as valuable doesn't mean others will, so one part of the time-management puzzle is ensuring that others don't manage our time for us.

Our perceptions of time will vary depending on the circumstances. Many of us will have said, at one time or another, something like, "I've been in this queue for hours" when in fact we've only been there five minutes, but the boredom has stretched those minutes out. At the other end of the spectrum, we often hear, "I don't know where the time went" or "The weekend flew by" after a fun event. The point is – and it's an important one for a manager to understand – it's highly unlikely that the individuals in our teams share the same perception of time as we do (at least not all of the time).

Let me ask you a question: how many times a day do you look at your watch? Can you make a guess? Do you have any idea at all? You probably don't know the answer to this question, which is absolutely normal. After all, you could look at your watch anywhere between 0 and 86,400 times a day.

However, most of us have a device capable of "giving us the time" on us or close to us, whether it's a phone, watch or clock. There's always information about time somewhere in our immediate environment. The physical measures of time are pretty much omnipresent.

Time is also extremely present in our everyday language. We often here, or even ask, "What time is it?", "Where's the time gone?" and "Doesn't time fly?" And the idea of performance is heavily related to time in today's society as we talk about the importance of objectives being time-bound.

In the workplace, we are obsessed with time all of the time. "When's the due date for that work?" we ask, or "When's this to be handed back?" or "How long is that meeting going to last? When do the quality or financial results come out? Do you have some time for me now?" I'm sure you get my drift.

I thought about all of this for a long time (no pun intended) before deciding to write on the subject. Why was that? Quite simply because so much has been written about time management that I wondered whether or not I could add anything useful. As I was thinking on this, it came to me that I had learned a tremendous amount about time during the course of my career – unfortunately, often the hard way. I've felt terrible stress due to time constraints of one kind or another – not just at work, either – and I'm far from being alone in this.

People are always trying to manage their time, but why do we talk about time management? Is time something that can be managed perfectly or even at all? Well, the short answer to this question is no. It cannot be managed perfectly due to its highly perishable nature. It can, however, be measured with a high degree of accuracy. You don't need a beautiful handmade Swiss watch to do so; any timepiece will do, although if you want the ultimate in precision, you will need an atomic clock.

Well, that's good news in itself, isn't it? As Tom DeMarco claims in his book *Software Creativity 2.0*:[1]

> *"You can't control what you can't measure."*

So, the fact that time can be measured means that it *can* be controlled or managed to some extent. Whether it is managed well or not is another matter entirely.

This is not a book exclusively about time management, though; it's also about finding how to manage or lead to make the best use of the time that we have at our disposal. In other words, to give ourselves time, we need to manage and lead in highly specific ways.

Build on the past, live for today and plan for tomorrow

These three concepts are of fundamental importance to leaders and managers. We as humans all learn from experience, both good and bad, but this is particularly important for leaders. In this context, we need to be continually learning about leadership and management and honing our skills because we are, after all, responsible for our people and their wellbeing.

Living for today ensures that we remain focused on both the task at hand and our people at all times. Planning for tomorrow is essential in light of the enormous worldwide changes which are ongoing in modern life (technology, climate change, natural resources running short etc). To adapt to change, we must first and foremost plan for it. As US Founding Father Benjamin Franklin has been credited with saying:

> *"If you fail to plan, you are planning to fail."*

To lead effectively, we need to use all three – the past, present and future – to their best effect. To do this, we must dedicate time to each one. In other words, we must have time to reflect upon the lessons we've learned in the past and what we are doing now, and to make plans to enable us to bring about our leadership vision of what the future will look like.

Success as a manager or leader doesn't depend only on what types of action we take, but also on how much time, and the quality of the time, we use to think things through. As it's so important to the success of leaders and managers, the concept of building on the past, living for today and planning for the future is fundamental to the content of this book. It shows that we must give adequate time to thinking about the most necessary and effective management and leadership styles to ensure that we use the time available to us in the optimum way. We will discuss the requirements for an optimal leadership agenda later in the introduction and in detail in the "What?" chapter of the book.

Optimum styles of management need to be directed not only towards our employees and subordinates, but also towards ourselves. After all, as leaders, we are managing our own time as well as our people's. And it's not just our time that we have to manage. We need to give consideration to our behaviours and attitudes, too. Failing to do so will inevitably lead to time lost in misunderstandings and poor communication with our team and the individuals within it.

Firefighting

Have you ever felt that you don't have enough time in the day to do everything you need to do? That there aren't enough hours and your work day is too short? Then when you get home and think back on your day, you have an all-too-familiar feeling that you've achieved nothing, but you can't figure out exactly what you did with your time.

This probably happens to all managers and leaders at one time or another. Depending on our workload and the demands the various stakeholders in the business, including our customers and employees, make on us, it could describe pretty much every day. However, if we find ourselves asking these questions on a regular basis, there is cause for concern.

One of the most common reasons we feel as if our day at work has slipped by without us achieving a fraction of what we'd hoped is that we have been doing what is commonly referred to as '"firefighting". This means we've been going from one problem or "fire" to another, trying to put each one out without ever dealing with their possible sources. But if all our time is being taken up by firefighting, how exactly do we go about finding and dealing with these sources?

Well, for a fire to spread, certain criteria need to be met. A fire needs three things to start and continue to burn:

> A source of heat or ignition (for example a match)
> Fuel (anything flammable)
> Oxygen

We can represent these elements in a triangle:

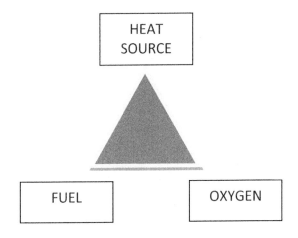

What has this got to do with how we use our time as a manager or leader? Well, let's think about it like this.

What are the three areas in business where time-wasting and procrastination can be the most damaging? In my view, the worst offenders are:

- ➢ The task itself
- ➢ Us: our habits and behaviours as managers and leaders
- ➢ The team (or individual people within the team).

You may be wondering why I have included managers or leaders in the triangle. Surely we aren't the architects of our own shortage of time, are we?

This section of the triangle tends to be more to do with how we manage upwards than downwards. It could be that we have difficulty saying no to our boss, even when what they're asking is impossible. Then we waste an enormous amount of time trying to do it in any case. We've all been there.

Like the elements that lead to a fire starting and spreading, let's represent the three reasons for lost time as a triangle:

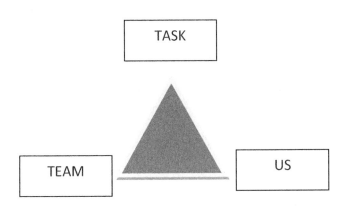

Unlike with fire, the solution is not to remove any or all of the sources from this triangle. What we need to analyse here is from which part of the triangle the most significant "time leaks" are springing. Are we losing time due to the way we are behaving or the way the team or individuals from the team are behaving? Is it because of how we're planning tasks? Perhaps it's down to a complete lack of planning. These are among the most important questions to ask ourselves if we are to become capable managers, able to use our time optimally.

Let's go into more depth, starting with the task. As a concrete example, let's say that the task is to build a house (no pun intended). Before we begin, we need to define certain things:

➤ **The scope.** What size will the house be? How many floors? How many rooms in total? How many bedrooms? Is there a garage? Garden? How big will the kitchen be?

➤ **The plan.** A precise plan of the layout of the house will be prepared by an architect and their team

➤ **The resources:**
  o Human resources
  o Financial resources
  o Physical resources
  o Intangible resources

If we don't define any of these points sufficiently, we will encounter problems in completing the task not only within a given time, but at all. For example, let's say that we haven't defined the scope in enough detail at the outset and find we need to build an extra bedroom and provide room in the garage for two cars instead of one. We'll lose time here because:

➤ The architect will have to make new plans
➤ We'll need to seek new planning permission from the local authorities, which can be a long process
➤ If the building work has already started, the builders will need to adapt or even demolish and rebuild certain parts of the house

Now let's assume that we have spent an adequate amount of time defining the scope, but the plan hasn't been drawn to scale correctly. We'll lose time here because:

- The builders will constantly need to make adjustments to rectify the inaccurate measurements
- We may have to decide to alter the scope due to a lack of space

Finally, we have a well-defined scope and the plans are drawn to scale with the perfect amount of detail required. Is there room for anything else to go wrong? Indeed there is. What about the resources available to us?

Human resources:

- Do we have enough people to build the house? Are they available when we want to do our project?
- Do we have the right people with the right skills to build the house: bricklayers, plumbers, electricians, carpenters, painters?
- Who's running the project? Us, the architect or a project manager?

Financial resources:

- How much is the total budget?
- What happens if the total budget is not respected?
- Do we have enough money for the project?
- How are we financing the project? Our own capital? Borrowing from a bank or another financial institution?

Physical resources:

> ➢ What quality or types of material will we use (for example, double or triple glazing for the windows)?
> ➢ Have we taken possible delays for the delivery of certain materials into account? Have we checked that these materials are even available?

There are an enormous number of questions we have to ask at this stage of the project. If we don't have the answers to all of them, we're likely to fall rapidly into difficulties regarding the overall goal of building our house.

This underlines how fundamental planning is to the successful completion of tasks. If the right people are not available at the right time, if we don't have the financial resources in place, if the materials are not available when we need them, it can cause delays. The knock-on effect of the delays could be that skilled people are no longer available when we finally get the project back on track.

This example is pertinent for all leaders and managers. We are responsible for ensuring that the tasks within our business or organisation are completed properly in a timely manner. It doesn't matter which industry we are talking about; as far as tasks go, we have to discuss the scope, the plan and the available resources. When we're a manager or leader, it is part of our role.

Let's take another example, this time from a service industry. Say you are managing a hotel and you've just been told that you need to increase the service quality by five points.

First of all, what is the scope here? Are you talking about the quality of service from all the guest-facing staff of the hotel? Are there specific areas that you need to focus on? Are there more service improvements required at the reception desk than in the restaurants?

Once you've defined the scope, what's the plan? Let's say you decide you need to retrain the staff at reception as the most important part of your strategy; the first question to ask now would be, what kind of training do they require? Is it language training? Is their level of English not good enough? Is it technical training because the check-in process is too slow? Is it service excellence training because you've had too many complaints about people on reception being rude or not giving a warm welcome to guests? Is it a mixture of all three? Once you've figured all of that out, you'll then need to know how many hours of training the reception staff require.

When you know the scope (the reception) and what kind of training and how many hours you need to provide (the plan), what about resources? Are there people in house who can deliver the training or are you going to use an outside company? If it's the latter, how much is it going to cost? Will you need to temporarily replace the reception staff while they are being trained? If so, how much will this cost? How much of the hotel's training budget is available for this?

Even the simplest of tasks can require a high degree of precision and definition. If you don't believe me, ask your team how to make a cup of tea one day. My good friend Jon Reece first told me about this exercise and I have tried it many times now. The results are always enlightening.

The simplest way to carry out this exercise is to ask each person in your team to describe in detail how to make the best cup of tea possible. The only rules are that they have five minutes to write their description and each person must do this entirely on their own. They then each describe to the rest of the group how to make a cup of tea.

The results and feedback I have witnessed from this exercise have been both hilarious and astonishing. Apparently, the perfect cup of tea needs to be made:

> ➤ With tea leaves; with teabags; with tea from different countries; with different brands
> ➤ In a pre-heated teapot; in a cold teapot; directly in a mug

➢ With milk; without milk; with lemon; without lemon

It's amazing the number of different ways a great cup of tea can be made. The point is that the task description at the beginning wasn't nearly precise enough. If people don't know whether the tea is to be made with tea leaves or teabags, in a teapot or directly in a mug, they will each default to their own separate ways of working

If we wish to avoid wasting time unnecessarily, all tasks need precision detail and planning. And the more complex the task, the more detailed the planning and the definition of scope need to be. The two words to keep in mind when we're defining any task are precision and clarity.

Let's now talk about the second part of our triangle: us, the leaders. Ask yourself, "Do I really make the best use of my time as a manager?" Use a sliding scale from 1 to 10 to establish how efficiently you use your time, 1 being the least efficiently and 10 being the most.

Most of us, if we're being honest, will not be at 10. We tend to spend too much time on:

➢ Informal meetings or conversations
➢ Thinking about lunch, tea break or the weekend
➢ Procrastinating

➤ Thinking about strategy on our own instead of planning it properly with others

I'm sure you could add many more things to this list. The reasons we don't use our time as efficiently as we could will differ depending on our own personal experience and our perceptions about time, what is and isn't important for us as a manager or leader, and our role within the organisation. The only constant is that there *will* be reasons why we're experiencing time leaks.

There are two things which are extremely important if we want to become more efficient in how we use our time:

➤ Self-discipline
➤ Leadership goals

Self-discipline is self-explanatory, but what exactly is a leadership goal? Arguably, there is only one leadership goal that matters in terms of effective time management and that is to be as people-focused as possible at all times. Make sure you plan for this.

It may seem strange that I have emphasised being people-focused considering the importance of the task itself, but the reason behind this will become crystal clear later in the book. It also leads us nicely on to the third part of the time-loss triangle: the team.

There are three main reasons why teams can lose valuable time:

> - They don't work well together or don't trust each other
> - They don't know what is expected of them as a team and/or don't have common goals
> - They don't have sufficient clarity as to what is expected from each individual on the team

These three points are interdependent. Fortunately for us, they are also easily resolved. They can only exist if the manager or leader has lost their focus on and understanding of their people. This leads inevitably to a lack of clarity.

Therefore, the main requirements for an optimal leadership agenda are:

> - Precision and clarity in the way that we communicate with our people
> - Self-discipline regarding our use of time. We need to lead by example
> - Being people-focused as opposed to task-focused

I have asked a lot of questions during this introduction. One of the best habits that a good leader can adopt is to ask themselves and their team the right questions.

What to expect from this book

We will be talking about two areas in this book:

- ➢ The most time-efficient and effective ways to lead (or to lose the least time)
- ➢ The most effective techniques to manage our own and other people's time

As I did in the first book of the series, *One to One: Manging quality time with individuals for engagement and success,* I will use a framework based on the use of the pertinent 5WH questions. The 5WH questions are:

- ➢ What?
- ➢ Why?
- ➢ When?
- ➢ Where?
- ➢ Who?
- ➢ How?

I use this framework to facilitate learning and give you an easy-to-follow and practical guide which will allow you to manage both your own and your people's time effectively. In doing so, you will create an ongoing agenda for effective leadership and a healthy work environment where all can thrive.

[1] Glass, RL; DeMarco, T (2006) *Software Creativity 2.0* (Developer Books, p. 130)

PART ONE – THE 5WS

WHAT

Time to Manage

An agenda for effective leadership

5WH

WHAT

What are we actually talking about when we're discussing managing time to create an agenda for effective leadership? Well, first and foremost it's about what to do to make the best use of our own time while ensuring that our people make the best use of theirs.

The Introduction emphasised three concepts:

- ➢ Precision and clarity in communication
- ➢ Self-discipline
- ➢ People-focused management

These are *what* we need for an optimal leadership agenda, but before we go on to discuss each of these areas in detail and define exactly what we mean in each case, first we need to talk about the "substance" that we are going to be manipulating: time itself. This will clarify how we are to view time as managers and leaders throughout the rest of the book.

The first two definitions of time in *The Merriam-Webster Dictionary* are:[1]

> *"The measured or measurable period during which an action, process, or condition exists or continues."*

And:

> *"A non-spatial continuum that is*
> *measured in terms of events which*
> *succeed one another from past*
> *through present to future."*

Two things are immediately obvious from these definitions: time *can* be measured, and the importance of the past, present and future. The latter ties in nicely with the concept we explored in the Introduction:

Build on the past, live for today and plan for tomorrow.

So, the basic answer to the "What?" question about time in the context of this book is that it's something that can be measured and has three phases: past, present and future. But as managers and leaders, how do we perceive what time is?

The best way for us to look at it is as a commodity. In fact, because of its finite nature and how perishable it is, it is by far our most important commodity.

If we then ask ourselves what we need to be using this commodity for, we can find the answer in the Introduction. We use our most important commodity, time, in the service of our most important asset, people.

To help us think more about our definitions of time and the decisions we need to take regarding our use of it, let's look at the concept of opportunity cost. An economist would say that our commodity, time, is a scarce resource (and it is). Like all scarce resources, it has demands made on it and is in finite supply. What, then, is opportunity cost and what is its relevance here?

When we decide to use our time to do one thing, we are simultaneously forgoing the opportunity to use this time to do something else. Let's illustrate a common workplace example: the cost to our time on the shop floor if we're caught up in meetings all day, and vice versa. In diagrammatic form, this would look something like:

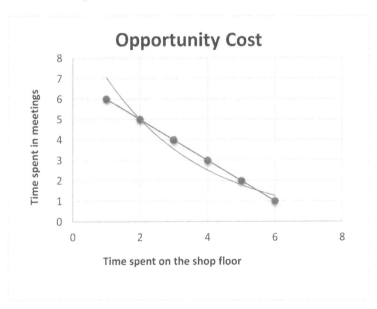

Opportunity Cost

Time spent in meetings (y-axis)

Time spent on the shop floor (x-axis)

It's clear that the amount of time we spend in meetings is inversely proportional to the amount of time we spend on the shop floor. If we spend five hours of a seven-hour working day in meetings, we will only spend two hours on the shop floor. The opportunity cost is therefore five hours on the shop floor lost.

If you pride yourself as someone who manages by walking around, but find you're spending a disproportionate amount of time in meetings, this will definitely be a source of frustration. The opportunity cost doesn't mean that meetings are not important – some meetings are absolutely crucial to the running of a business or organisation – but it does mean that what you choose to do with your time as a manager or leader is absolutely fundamental to your success. Never underestimate it.

Planning your leadership agenda means deciding what exactly to spend the majority of your time on. Is that meeting really crucial? Do you have to attend or could a team member be an equally effective attendee? Do you need to spend so many hours on the shop floor? Do the employees appreciate the time you dedicate to them or is it straying into the realms of micromanaging?

Now let's look at the three areas of an optimal leadership agenda in more detail. These areas are fundamental to effective management of both your and your people's time. We'll start with precision and clarity.

Precision and clarity in communication

The methods that we use to communicate with our teams and the individuals in those teams need to be as participative as possible in nature. This will ensure that as managers, we are in a position not only to lead our people, but also to reassure them when necessary and build relationships based on confidence and trust, one conversation at a time.

There are so many ways to communicate with groups and individuals that we are in some ways spoiled for choice. For example, some situations require us merely to relay or share information rather than enter into conversation. If our people need a bit more clarification, a short question-and-answer session at the end of a meeting will generally suffice. At the other end of the spectrum, a yearly appraisal interview requires detailed preparation based on two-way communication.

Whatever type of communication a given situation requires, you must always ensure that you are speaking a language the group or individual concerned understands. Be careful of using too much jargon, or if you are using jargon, make sure that it's appropriate. In other words, it needs to be as familiar to those you're addressing at that particular time as it is to you.

Another extremely important element in your communication "toolbox" is reformulation. This practice in a conversation of repeating what someone has said to you back to them in your own words, and asking if they agree, allows you to check with them that you have understood perfectly. I recommend you develop a habit of asking questions along the lines of: "Let's just check I have understood you – you are saying A, B and C. Is that correct?"

Last, but by no means least, is the fundamental importance of asking people the right questions (including yourself when you are problem solving). We all know how to ask questions, but if the answer to each question that we ask is a simple yes or no, communicating effectively is going to become impossible.

For example, if you ask someone, "Are you happy at work?" the answer is likely to be yes or no. This will not provide you with much useful information to carry on the conversation and find out more. If, on the other hand, you ask, "What is it that you are enjoying most about your work at the moment?" or "What efforts do we need to make to improve your current working conditions?" these open questions tend to elicit valuable information.

Given what you learned in the Introduction, it will likely come as no surprise that the most important questions to have front of mind begin with:

- ➤ What?
- ➤ Why?
- ➤ When?
- ➤ Where?
- ➤ Who?
- ➤ How?

In asking these questions, you ensure that you know precisely what you and the people you are addressing are talking about.

That said, effective communication is not just about precision. It's also about motivation. Let's leave "What?" for a couple of minutes and take the why and how questions as examples. After all, we know what we're aiming for in this context: motivation.

It's easy to see that "Why?" is important when it comes to motivation. When people know why they are doing something – they understand there is a reason or a purpose to what they are doing – they are much more likely to be motivated to do it to the best of their ability.

The "How?" question in this context relates, of course, to how you or your people will carry out a specific task. If you want your people to do something, but don't dedicate enough time and resources to training them how to do it, this will affect their motivation negatively. It will also clearly affect their productivity and leave them extremely frustrated by the situation. This generally leads to two outcomes: a toxic environment as demotivated employees look for an outlet for their frustration, and a high staff turnover. As a result, you're back to firefighting all the time.

All of the questions we will cover in the chapters of this book are extremely important if you wish to have a participative approach to communication at work based on the most effective use of collective intelligence. After all, two heads are better than one, so just imagine what a roomful of heads all communicating effectively can achieve.

We will come back to how and why in the relevant chapters. For now, let's return to what. What is the importance of self-discipline?

Self-discipline

This means having the necessary discipline to establish rules, habits and methods of working to ensure that we give sufficient time to planning while eliminating the root causes of time-wasting. Self-discipline also covers how we function best under any given circumstances.

It is essential to manage ourselves well with regards to time and lead by example. More than this, though, it is critical that we don't allow our own "battery" to become depleted. As in any area of life, if we are too tired or unhealthy to function correctly in the workplace, this will adversely affect our performance. And those that we work with will soon pick up on this.

Make sure, before you even think about managing the performance of others, that you are giving enough time to looking after number one – yourself. I am not talking about work-life balance here; I believe this as a general concept to be a myth. Every individual has to find their own balance; there is no "one size fits all" which is optimal for everyone.

For some people, their whole life revolves around their work and their vision of what they want to achieve through their work. For others, work is only a way of making a living. In other words, some people live to work while others work to live, and there are many people who fall somewhere in between these two extremes. No approach is wrong if it's right for that individual, so everyone has to find their own personal balance between how much time they spend with their family, friends, hobbies, sporting activities and how much time they're willing and happy to spend at work.

So if you've got to find your own balance, what exactly is my reason for including this here? Once you have found the balance that best suits you, make sure you have the self-discipline to respect it as well as you can. It is essential to look after your own health and wellbeing to ensure that you are mentally and physically fit enough to work, manage and lead. The simple truth is if you don't look after yourself, no one is going to do it for you.

You may have met people who say that they only need four hours of sleep a night to function at their optimum level. Former UK Prime Minister Margaret Thatcher was a famous example of someone who made this claim,[2] but personally, I need eight. Major clinical studies indicate that all adults need between seven and nine hours sleep every night, and that people like the late Baroness Thatcher who only require four hours are incredibly rare.[3] In most cases, they aren't performing optimally at all; they are actually damaging their own health.[4] It would appear that the old adage "Early to bed and early to rise, makes a man healthy, wealthy, and wise"[5] is pretty accurate.

That's all very well, but here's another "What?" for you: "What about people who suffer with insomnia?" How soul destroying it must be to know you need a good eight hours' sleep, to crave a night of unbroken rest, but instead lie awake, watching your precious commodity time slip away hour after hour until the insomnia itself becomes the root of the anxiety keeping you awake. If this resonates with you, what can you do to break this cycle?

Fear not – here are some tips that worked for a former insomniac I know, and if you give them a go, they may well work for you too:

- Avoid caffeine (pretty obvious) and alcohol (not so obvious), especially in the hours leading up to bedtime.
- Avoid blue light, such as that which shines from computer monitors, TVs, phones etc. If you want to watch TV or use your electronic device before bedtime, I recommend you invest in a pair of blue-light blockers. You can wear these like sunglasses, or get some that you clip over your everyday spectacles.
- Eat a few hours before bedtime, especially if you enjoy a cooked meal in the evening, to give your system plenty of time for digestion.
- Exercise daily, but not just before you go to bed as you will still be buzzing with endorphins. A brisk walk, a run, a cycle ride, a swim, especially out in the fresh air, does wonders for a relaxing night's sleep.

Many people practise meditation to help to stop their minds racing in the small hours of the morning. There are plenty of apps such as Calm[6] if you fancy giving this a try and need some guidance.

Along with a decent night's sleep and making sure that you get appropriate and timely medical attention if you feel you have any health issues, what else do you need to make sure you're in tip-top condition? A healthy diet is, of course, paramount. Simply cutting down on your sugar intake can do wonders for your energy levels.

This is all pretty basic stuff. Most of us know how to stay healthy in theory, but what's important is to put this knowledge into practice.

But what exactly is the reason it's so important that you look after yourself first and foremost? Imagine, for a moment, that you are in an aeroplane that's making an emergency landing out at sea and breathable air is in short supply. Whose oxygen mask do you put on first? Do you help your children, or your spouse, or your friends, or the person in the seat next to you to put theirs on, and then deal with your own? Of course not: you put on your own mask first so that you will be in a position (i.e. not unconscious) to help other people.

It's the same thing for you as a manager in your working environment. Make sure that you are in a position to help your team and the individuals in your team by looking after yourself first. If you're not performing at your optimum levels, there's little chance that your team will be either. Never forget that as the leader, you are always under the microscope. In other words, your team members are constantly looking to you as an example to follow.

Self-discipline is not only about self-care to be at your best in terms of work performance. It's also to do with self-control. You need to maintain a balanced approach at all times, behaving towards others as you'd expect them to behave towards you. For example, a self-disciplined manager will remain calm however difficult a situation might be.

It goes without saying that you won't always be feeling calm inside. On the contrary, you may feel at times as if your head is about to explode because there are so many things happening at once. What's important is that you have the self-discipline to make sure your team members do not see this. No throwing things, shouting or swearing, unless you're absolutely sure no one can see or hear you doing it.

Practising self-discipline and leading by example are part and parcel of our role, but what about the advice that tells us that as modern managers and leaders, we should always be ourselves? This is true to a certain extent, but the fact remains that we do have a role to play. We may not always be feeling 100%, but if we are insisting that all of our client-facing staff must smile and give the perfect welcome to our customers, for example, we need to be doing exactly the same with them.

So far, we've established that self-discipline is to do with self-care and self-control. Last but not least, it's to do with the rules that we impose on ourselves with regard to the way that we choose to work and inspire others towards achieving their goals. In other words, it's to do with planning our work then working our plan.

We will come back to planning when we reach the "How?" section of the book. Suffice to say for the moment that plans in themselves are of absolutely no use if they are not translated into action at some point.

People-focused management

Broadly speaking, this is about two things. First and foremost, truly care for your people and regard them as internal customers. Secondly, ensure that you spend adequate time with your teams in the right way.

Basically, people-focused management is not about doing things right (efficiency); it's much more to do with using our time to do the right things (effectiveness), and ensuring that we have mechanisms in place within the organisation that allow people opportunities to express themselves and feel they have a real purpose in the workplace. Our job as leaders is to create conditions for all of our people to perform to the absolute best of their abilities. As we saw in the Foreword, these conditions are to do with both the physical and social environments at work.

As leaders, we need to pay due attention to our employee satisfaction or engagement surveys and become experts in employee relationship management (ERM). Far too often, managers and leaders in organisations spend huge amounts of time on analysing customer feedback and figuring out how to increase customer loyalty, while only giving minimal attention to employee engagement. It's no good improving the menu in the canteen, for example, and then shoving the staff survey in the drawer (or the bin) till next year and ignoring all the rest of the feedback. I'm sure you have an idea what I'm talking about here, right?

As a leader and manager, you need to keep your focus on your employees. These are your most important customers, so build and maintain strong relationships with your people based on mutual confidence and trust. This is the essence of people-focused management and will lead to a workforce that is motivated, has purpose and thrives in the working environment that you create together. People always come first; it's not just a fancy slogan describing company culture, but part of the DNA of optimal leadership.

Now we know what the main requirements for an optimal leadership agenda are and what role they play, as we go forward, we will be discussing how best to use people-focused management, self-discipline and clear, precise communication in effective leadership. This will permit us both to manage and to use our time in the best possible way and create a healthy environment where everyone can find purpose and thrive.

[1] *The Merriam-Webster Dictionary* www.merriam-webster.com/dictionary/time

[2] de Castella, T (10 April 2013) "Thatcher: Can people get by on four hours' sleep?" (*BBC News Magazine*) www.bbc.co

[3] Chaput, JP; Dutil, C; Sampasa-Kanyinga, H (2018) "Sleeping hours: what is the ideal number and how does age impact this?" (*Nature and Science of Sleep*, 10, pp. 421–430) https://doi.org/10.2147/NSS.S163071

[4] MedlinePlus "Healthy sleep" https://medlineplus.gov/healthysleep.html

[5] Speake, J (2015) *Oxford Dictionary of Proverbs* (Sixth edition, Oxford University Press)

[6] Calm: Sleep and Meditation app www.calm.com

WHY

Time to Manage

An agenda for effective leadership

5WH

WHY

The question "Why?" is fundamental to everything we do in our lives to such an extent that if we don't know the answer, we often feel lost. By lost, I mean without purpose, and without purpose, we will find it extremely difficult to have any meaningful motivation either intrinsically or extrinsically.

People need to know why they are doing something – especially if they're required to do it in a certain way – if they are to perform to the best of their ability. Indeed, you will not be able to thrive as a manager or leader without knowing why you are a leader or manager. The absence of clear purpose will result in a lack of vision, and your people are counting on you to be the one not only to provide vision, but also to "show the way" with guidance through the setting of clear goals and objectives.

Imagine how chaotic it would be to lead or act or have others act without purpose, vision and clear goals. You would then have no strategy to move forward, no clear tactics in place; people would be floundering around in circles, all following their own different paths (remember all the ways to make a cup of tea?) and getting nowhere.

This quote from Sun Tzu's *Art of War* sums it up nicely:[1]

> *"Strategy without tactics is the slowest route to victory. Tactics without strategy is the noise before defeat."*

To put it simply, you will be the "blind leading the blind" with no strategy or tactics in place. In a workplace situation, this would have disastrous consequences for all concerned.

To highlight this, let's imagine a hospital's Accident and Emergency (A&E) department with no system of triage. Triage comes from the French word *trier,* which means sorting or organising, and is essential in busy A&E departments (as well as in war zones) to ensure the people most in need of medical intervention are treated first.

A friend in the medical profession explained to me how the basic triage system works. The colour red is used to signify the most urgent cases where patients are in life-threatening situations and require immediate treatment. Yellow signifies that the patient is not in immediate danger, but will soon require treatment. Green represents less serious injuries that will eventually require treatment. Black sadly means that the person is beyond help and all that the medical team can do is to make them as comfortable as possible.

Without this type of system in place, medical staff would stand little chance of making optimal decisions under the most difficult of circumstances. Even with triage, the healthcare professionals in an A&E department work under tremendous levels of stress. If there were no type of system for them to follow, the consequences would likely be disastrous for all concerned (particularly the patients).

Although the consequences of managers and leaders in business making wrong decisions aren't going to be a matter of life or death, pressure in the form of time constraints and priorities does exist for us. For this reason, many organisational leaders use colour-coded "traffic light" systems when assessing the relative risks of different choices.

As with traffic lights on the roads, red means stop. The route we're contemplating will lead us and our people nowhere, so we don't take it. But this means we still have to make a decision on another direction or we will freeze in place.

Green, on the other hand, means go – but we need to be aware that this route is not without danger. If we speed into the sunset without giving any regard to what's going on around us – in other words, we've not weighed up all the potential risks – there's a chance we will crash, making this the wrong path to take too.

The best approach is amber. We proceed down this route, but remain aware of the risks, and at all times we are ready either to stop and change direction or to go for it.

The purpose – the why – behind everything we do, every decision we make, is of utmost importance in leadership as it will drive both us and our people towards optimal performance. Being clear on our why is the only way our management style can be truly people-focused. With people-focused management in mind, let's now have a look at why the two pillars that support it are of equally critical importance.

Why self-discipline?

In the last chapter, we talked about people-focused management supported by the pillars of self-discipline and clear, precise communication. Why, exactly, are these two pillars so important?

To look at this in more detail, let's imagine situations in which we remove one of the pillars. If we remove self-discipline, it's easy to see that we will not be as efficient or effective in whatever it is that we do. In addition, and just as importantly, our people will pick up on this and are likely to imitate our behaviour, which will ultimately lead to overall dysfunction for the organisation that will be hard to repair in the future.

As managers and leaders, we need to set a great example in terms of self-discipline. It takes years to build a reputation, but only minutes to destroy it. In a business setting, this is particularly true for leaders as we're the people everyone else is following.

Discipline is also important in the strictest sense of the term. We aren't going to accept behaviours from our people that we would not accept from ourselves, are we? So, if we're seeing such behaviours from some of our people, even though we ourselves are modelling the behaviours that align with the company or organisation's culture and values, we have to deal with them swiftly and thoroughly.

Make no mistake, I'm not talking about a lack of tolerance here; I'm talking about fairness. We must not allow behaviour which is toxic or damaging to the organisation to go unpunished or spread. If we do, we run the risk of our good employees (the vast majority) either adopting these behaviours or leaving. Either way, this will prove damaging for business.

Virtually nothing affects staff morale and motivation as adversely as seeing bad behaviour tolerated by management, which is why it's essential we're seen to deal with it fairly and immediately. We all know what happens when we leave a "rotten apple" in the barrel. General and self-discipline are equally necessary to lead an organisation that demonstrates good practice, fairness and the same rules for everyone.

Why clear communication?

Now we know why discipline is essential, we surely won't be removing that pillar. But why are effective methods of communication of equal importance?

Nature does not exist in a vacuum, so if as managers we create a leadership communication vacuum, our people will fill it. What will they fill it with, though? Probably one or more of:

- ➢ Rumours
- ➢ Miscommunication
- ➢ Refusal to share vital information with other teams
- ➢ Misunderstandings
- ➢ Social problems
- ➢ Unnecessary and time-wasting conflicts

And this list is by no means exhaustive.

You don't want any of these to enter into your organisation. Why not? Because the likely consequences will be both your managerial control and staff morale being diminished or even lost completely. Unsubstantiated gossip can be extremely destructive not only for people on an individual basis, but for the organisation as a whole.

If you want to imagine why this is, take a minute to think about any of the points on the list happening in your personal life. Imagine the consequences, and then multiply them to translate them to a workplace situation.

If you are no longer communicating with your employees, they will find others who will listen. These others may be your customers or future recruits. Imagine the effect on customer loyalty or onboarding good staff if all your people are moaning and groaning and spreading false rumours about your organisation.

Why is customer and employee loyalty so important? If you don't have it, far from being able to plan and manage your time, you will yet again be firefighting, dividing your most precious commodity between trying (and probably failing) to attract the best employees and trying (and probably failing) to gain and keep custom flowing into your company or organisation.

Communication and discipline are equally essential pillars to support people-focused management. As we can see, the consequences of removing either would be serious and severely damage our ability to manage our time in the optimum way. But why exactly is people-focused management so important?

Why people-focused management?

Without people-focused management and the pillars that support it, we create unnecessary levels of stress for the organisation and the individuals who work there. But why exactly does stress occur?

If we were to spend some of our valuable time researching the biggest causes of stress in society, we probably wouldn't be particularly surprised with the results. Separate articles by Neil Schneiderman[2] and Elizabeth Scott PhD[3] talk about the following as being among the principal sources of stress:

➢ Money
➢ Work
➢ Health

These three causes of stress are very much interrelated. They also take us neatly back to the question "Why?"

Why does money cause stress for so many people? The answer is quite simple, really: we need money to support ourselves and maybe our families in our current society. In other words, even before we start thinking about treats like holidays and nights out, we need money for our basic needs such as food and shelter.

Why are money and work interrelated? This is another one that's easy to answer: to make money, we need to work. But where does health fit in?

As we saw in the "What?" chapter, we need to be healthy enough (both physically and mentally) to work to the best of our abilities. And if we're not working to the best of our abilities, we're unlikely to be able to maintain a work position that will pay us enough to support ourselves, let alone anyone else.

The three main causes of stress are not only interrelated, they're cyclic, so we can quickly find ourselves in a descending spiral. The stress of not having enough money leads us to push ourselves to the limits at work and never take a break, which inevitably results in health problems leading to loss of work, leading to lack of money. The resultant stress levels will result in a further loss of health, and down we go.

I've heard people say that a certain amount of stress is healthy. If by stress they mean having ambitious personal or work goals, I would tend to agree with this, but constant high levels of stress are always detrimental to our health.

Here are some of the more common manifestations of stress over a prolonged period:[4]

- ➢ Aches
- ➢ Chest pains

- ➢ Exhaustion, often caused by insomnia
- ➢ Headaches, dizziness or shaking
- ➢ High blood pressure
- ➢ Muscle tension or jaw clenching
- ➢ Stomach pains and digestive problems
- ➢ Depression and anxiety

Unfortunately, some people have a tendency to compound these problems by trying to reduce symptoms in unhealthy ways such as excessive smoking, drinking or drug abuse. You don't need to be a healthcare professional to see how any of these will exacerbate rather than cure the problem. Should you find yourself suffering from any of these symptoms, I would urge you to seek professional medical assistance as quickly as possible.

I'm sure we can all agree that taking preventive measures regarding stress is important. In this book, you will learn how to reduce stress for managers and leaders. You will become equipped with the necessary tools to manage both efficiently (doing things well) and effectively (doing the right things) while maintaining a healthy working environment for all your people. You'll likely be amazed at how much of your most valuable commodity, time, you will then have at your disposal.

---

[1] Tzu, Sun *The Art of War* (Capstone Classics, 2010)

[2] Schneiderman, N; Ironson, G; Siegel, SD (27 April 2005) "Stress and Health: Psychological, behavioral, and biological determinants" (*Annual Review of Clinical Psychology*) https://www.annualreviews.org/doi/10.1146/annurev.clinpsy.1.102803.144141?url_ver=Z39.88-2003&rfr_id=ori%3Arid%3Acrossref.org&rfr_dat=cr_pub%3Dpubmed

[3] Scott, E (23 May 2022) "The Main Causes of Stress" (Very Well Mind) https://www.verywellmind.com/what-are-the-main-causes-of-stress-3145063

[4] Yaribeygi, H; Panahi, Y; Sahraei, H; Johnston, TP; Sahebkar, A (2017) "The impact of stress on body function: A review" (National Library of Medicine) www.ncbi.nlm.nih.gov/pmc/articles/PMC5579396

WHEN

Time to Manage

An agenda for effective leadership

5WH

WHEN

I'm sure we've all heard the expression "There's a time and place for everything." Elaborating on this, I would propose that there's a time and a place for everything, whether it's important, urgent, neither or both.

When people talk about work-life balance, they tend to mean it in terms of how much time on average they dedicate to different areas of their lives. I am not a great believer in this approach at all because each of us has a different balance. Some of us enjoy our work more than anything else; others prioritise leisure time with our family or friends or on our own.

I invite you to do this exercise. First of all, draw a circle. Then divide it up into the following segments:

- ➤ Working
- ➤ Sleeping
- ➤ Family and friends
- ➤ Time for yourself/leisure
- ➤ Obligations (paperwork, shopping, dentist or doctor appointments, etc)

Give the biggest portion of the circle to the area you spend the most time on and the smallest to where you spend the least time. Endeavour to construct your circle to illustrate the amount of time you really spend on each of the areas.

Take a short coffee break, and then draw a new circle without looking at the first one. This time, you want the divisions within your circle to represent the amount of time you would ideally like to spend on each of the areas.

Don't be surprised if you end up with two circles which look significantly different to one another. If this is the case, it's not necessarily a cause for concern in and of itself, but if the fact that the two circles don't match becomes a source of stress for you, then you may want to look at how you can align them.

To do this, have a look at when you can spend more of your time doing what you enjoy and less doing what you don't enjoy so much. Even if you're in the habit of doing certain things in a certain way at a certain time, you can change it. This comes down to self-discipline.

When to sleep

Let's take the simple example of sleeping and working. Some people are capable of working an enormous number of hours and sleeping very few without damaging their health in any way. If you are one of these people, you are lucky indeed; most of us need between seven and nine hours' sleep every night.

We touched on some ways to combat insomnia in the "What" chapter. There is also a lot of research into what is known as sleep hygiene.[1] Basically, this means the optimal conditions that lead to us getting the hours of sleep we need:

> - Minimise light and noise disruption as much as possible
> - Have the same sleep schedule for weekdays and weekends. In other words, when you go to bed and get up on a Saturday is the same as when you do so on a Monday
> - Stop using your electronic devices at least half an hour before you go to bed. As we discovered earlier in the book, you can wear blue-light blockers if you simply have to use an electronic device close to bedtime, but it's better, if possible, to avoid blue light altogether in the run-up to settling down to sleep
> - Make sure you have a comfortable bed and pillows
> - Sleep at the correct temperature (more on this coming up)
> - Update your to-do list at least one hour before you go to bed, then put it in a drawer and forget about it

The majority of these points are self-explanatory, but let's have a closer look at sleeping at the correct temperature. An enormous amount of research has been carried out into this in many different countries, including the US, Canada and the UK. The statistics recommend that the optimal temperature for sleeping is between 16 and 19 degrees Celsius (60–67 degrees Fahrenheit).[2]

Are you surprised by this? I was when I first saw it, but nevertheless, I made sure that I would sleep at a temperature of 19 degrees Celsius every night and am happy to say that I am now waking up much more refreshed and able to focus on what I am doing throughout the course of the day than I used to be.

During summer months, I maintain this temperature by keeping the blinds and doors to the bedroom closed during the day and airing the bedroom in the evening. In the winter, I simply ensure that the thermostat is set to 19 degrees at least two hours before going to bed.

If you are feeling exhausted when you awake and unable to focus during the day when you're at work, getting the right amount of quality sleep clearly needs to become a priority for you. If you try all the tips and advice I have shared here and earlier in the book and none of them works for you, please consult a doctor as quickly as possible. Sleep is crucially important.

So, now that we have established the optimum amount of time we need to sleep and how to make sure we get good quality sleep when we go to bed, what about the optimum amount of time to work in a day?

When to work

The average working day in North America and Europe is around eight hours and has been for some time. Let's take a brief look at where the concept of working eight hours a day five days a week came from.

The Welsh textile mill owner and social reformer Robert Owen is credited as the first person to call for eight hours of labour, eight hours of recreation and eight hours of rest each day for workers in the early 19th century.[3] On 25 September 1926, Henry Ford announced the eight-hour five-day work week in his famous motor company, while many other factories had their workers on more than eight hours a day and working six days a week.[45] Like Robert Owen, Ford strongly believed that people need time for both rest and recreation. It was not until 1938, though, with the signing of the Fair Labour Standards Act by Franklin Roosevelt, that workers in the United States had to be paid overtime if they worked more than forty hours a week.[6]

It may seem surprising that the number of hours people work on average per week has not much changed since the early 20th century, so maybe Robert Owen wasn't that far off when he called for eight hours' labour, eight hours' recreation and eight hours' rest (sleep). What has reduced dramatically is the total number of hours worked in a year for the vast majority of North Americans and Europeans with the introduction of paid holidays.

Far from increasing our output, working too many hours can adversely affect our productivity. If we take a circle and divide it into three equal segments to represent Robert Owen's suggestion, it would look like this:

The optimal division of our days is equal segments of work, sleep and leisure. If our days aren't divided equally in this way, we really need to work on this.

The eight hours of "recreation" is possibly misleadingly named as a lot of things need to go into this segment, and these things will look significantly different for each of us. They could include:

> Administrative tasks (tax returns and other paperwork, particularly if we're self-employed)

- ➢ Domestic chores (cleaning the house, ironing clothes, shopping etc)
- ➢ Quality time with family
- ➢ Quality time for ourselves (sports, hobbies etc)
- ➢ Self-care (seeing the doctor or dentist, keeping fit, relaxation, yoga etc)

As I'm sure you'll realise, this list is by no means exhaustive and it's not meant to be. But it does underline the fact that in the so-called "recreation" section there are a number of things which are quite simply hard work. They're obligations or chores that plain need to be done outside of our work hours.

This is another reason why I do not believe that there is a perfect work-life balance for all. However people spend their time when they're not at work and not asleep is their choice and theirs alone. The balance between personal obligations and true leisure time will be different for everyone, but one thing to remember is this:

We must under no circumstances sacrifice our sleep time for either work or leisure.

If we were to do this on a regular basis, we would be in no condition to be an effective leader in the workplace. This leads us on to our next chapter, which talks about *where* to spend our time and how to achieve this. Once again, though, remember you must find your own balance and stick to it.

[1] Fry, A; Rehman, A (29 April 2022) "What is Healthy Sleep?" (Sleep Foundation) https://www.sleepfoundation.org/sleep-hygiene/what-is-healthy-sleep

[2] Pacheco, D; Wright, H (2022) "The Best Temperature for Sleep" (Sleep Foundation) www.sleepfoundation.org/bedroom-environment/best-temperature-for-sleep#:~:text=The%20best%20bedroom%20temperature%20for, for%20the%20most%20comfortable%20sleep

[3] Debs, EV (August 1911) "The Eight Hour Work Day" (Internet Archive, 2006. Source: *International Socialist Review*, Vol XII, No. 2) https://www.marxists.org/archive/debs/works/1911/8hrday.htm

[4] Brinkley, D (31 March 2003) "The 40-H*Time Magazine*) https://content.time.com/time/specials/packages/article/0,28804,1977881_1977883_1977922,00.html

[5] Jacobson, L (9 September 2015) "Does the 8-Hour Day and the 40-Hour Week Come From Henry Ford, or Labor Unions?" (The Poynter Institute) https://www.politifact.com/factchecks/2015/sep/09/viral-image/does-8-hour-day-and-40-hour-come-henry-ford-or-lab/

[6] "Fair Labor Standards Act" (United States, 1938) (*Britannica*) https://www.britannica.com/event/Fair-Labor-Standards-Act

WHERE

Time to Manage

An agenda for effective leadership

5WH

WHERE

The importance of being organised has been around for a long time. Let's take as an example the ancient Chinese concept of Feng Shui, which works on the premise that the way the things in our houses are arranged has a direct impact on our happiness and success, and even our health. This is probably where the expression "getting our house in order" to mean sorting our lives out comes from.

Being clear with yourself and your employees on where exactly time needs to be spent in the organisation, and equally where not to spend time, is extremely important if you are to avoid wasting this precious commodity on pointless or meaningless tasks and/or discussions. This is called setting boundaries.

For example, many managers declare, "I have an open-door policy." You may have done so yourself, but without clarifying exactly where you mean this to apply, you might find yourself overwhelmed by people using your office in pointless ways. There'll be a constant stream of team members at your door, saying things like, "I just need a quick chat with you, boss," or "Could you give your opinion on this?" when the team member is perfectly capable of deciding for themselves, or "A few minutes of your time to go over my presentation..." Sound familiar? And before you know it, you're back to your days – your precious time

– passing you by without you achieving any, let alone all of your goals.

The lesson here is to be in charge of where you are using your time in the workplace rather than letting others take charge of it. Going back to the open-door policy example, I've often stated clearly to people in my teams that my door is always open "unless it's closed". If you want to be in charge of where you spend your time while at work, you need to make sure you express your boundaries explicitly rather than implicitly.

Key performance indicators

Something that will clearly show you where you need to spend your time is your key performance indicators (KPIs). Let's imagine for a moment that you are in an industry where there is a lot of competition to recruit the best talent possible. If this is the case, one of your most important company KPIs will be staff turnover.

If a normal staff turnover for your industry is around 6% per annum, woe betide your HR partner if they announce that staff turnover in your company is actually at 15% for the last year. And not only that, but the trend is on the increase.

Obviously, to address this KPI in the short term, you will need to increase your recruitment and training budget to replace the people who have been leaving with the best talent available.

Under these circumstances, as a leader you are then going to be spending a fair amount of your time with the HR team to resolve the attrition problem. But where would you start analysing and solving this problem?

I would suggest that one of the best places to start your analysis would be the exit interview information. Go through all the recent data with the HR team to identify the most "frequent" reasons departing staff have given for leaving. And if you don't have an exit interview process in place, you need to instigate one, and fast.

For the sake of this example, though, let's imagine that you have a very good system of exit interviews that are consistently carried out by qualified professionals in your HR team. When you examine the feedback from departing employees, you see the following reasons for leaving cropping up over and over:

> I can earn a much better salary for the same job elsewhere
> There are no promotion prospects or career planning opportunities in place here. Promotions always go to people from outside, so there's no policy of internal promotion
> I never see my manager, except when they come to criticise, and they don't listen to what I am saying in response

> ➤ My yearly evaluation was a joke! My manager didn't even give me any clear objectives for the coming year

Armed with this list, you can check whether or not the salaries, conditions, opportunities and benefits that you are offering are in line with the current market conditions. If you discover that you are, for example, offering a salary that's 20% below market, you are going to have to fix this immediately for both your current staff and the talent you are trying to attract. If you don't, you run the risk of aggravating an already unhealthy situation.

Then you are going to need to reconsider your policies and procedures with regard to internal promotion and career planning. On top of that, it would appear that at least some of your managers are operating at a distance from their reports rather than building relationships based on mutual trust and confidence, judging by the problems your organisation seems to be having with both daily people management and yearly appraisal interviews.

The likely conclusions from this staff turnover KPI and the investigation that it has led to are that you need succession or career planning in place, your evaluation and appraisal process is not designed correctly, your managers have not been trained properly on how to carry out their duties and your company isn't paying enough to retain top talent.

Knowing exactly where the problems lie, you can then speak to your teams and put in place clear objectives to resolve them.

Let's take another example of a KPI. This time, your company is losing market share and is in danger of having to close some of its production facilities. The team to spend time with here is sales and marketing. And the first thing you are going to have to talk about with them is whether the issue is purely price based or more to do with quality and design.

Let's say that you discover all of your main competitors are selling more volume than you worldwide. There could be numerous reasons for this. Here are some examples:

> Your main market is in the Americas and your competitors' websites are all in both Spanish and English, while your website is in English only

> When you do a Google search for your product using some generic key words, you are nowhere to be found while all of your main competitors appear on the first page

> Your mobile application is incredibly slow compared to your competitors'. When you do a test buy, it's both faster and easier on all of your competitors' sites

> ➤ All of your competitors' have a massive presence on social media and you have hardly any at all

It would seem in this example that there is an enormous amount of work to be done with your IT and marketing departments. To improve both your visibility and effectiveness dramatically in terms of e-commerce, you would need to:

> ➤ Ensure that you have a Spanish version of your website
> ➤ Look at how you are going to improve your search-engine optimisation (SEO) and search-engine marketing (SEM)
> ➤ Re-engineer your mobile application so that it works properly
> ➤ Put in place a community management team to expand your presence on social media and set up distribution channels and e-commerce connected to your social media profiles and website

These examples demonstrate how examining the main problems in your business – such as high staff turnover and insufficient market share – show you where you need to be going into more depth. And it's KPIs that show you where the problems are in the first place. But how do you know which KPIs are the correct ones to measure?

How to choose the right KPIs

To ensure that you are as effective as possible in discovering where problems may lie within your organisation, you must measure the right things. Basically, your KPIs must allow you to make a *diagnostic* of your organisation's health based on measurement of criteria that indicate both over and under performance in a certain number of predetermined areas.

Fortunately, there are certain KPIs which are universal in nature and synonymous with business success or failure. These include:

- ➢ Increasing or decreasing revenues
- ➢ Increasing or decreasing profits
- ➢ Healthy or unhealthy cash flow
- ➢ Increasing or decreasing market share
- ➢ Customer satisfaction improving or worsening
- ➢ Employee satisfaction improving or worsening

Even with this simple scorecard approach, you can propose a diagnostic at a given point in time. I recommend you do this with sufficient frequency (weekly, or at least monthly) to allow for adjustments to be made. Basically, much like you would find in an aircraft, you are giving yourself a dashboard which will allow you to pilot the organisation. Your KPIs should be telling you whether or not you are on course to meet the overall objectives of the organisation.

What would the pilot of a commercial aircraft be looking at most of the time on their instrument panel? I would suggest:

- ➢ The weight of the aircraft at the beginning of the voyage
- ➢ The height the aircraft is flying at
- ➢ The amount of fuel the aircraft needs to reach its destination
- ➢ The speed the aircraft needs to travel at to arrive at its destination in time
- ➢ Weather instruments and information to predict and possibly avoid areas of turbulence
- ➢ Global positioning
- ➢ Information from air-traffic control
- ➢ The direction of the aircraft

All this information relates to the aircraft arriving at the destination *in a safe and timely manner*. This is the goal of the aircraft pilot. The measurement of these KPIs – making sure they are as the pilot would expect them to be – will allow them to achieve this goal or take remedial action if the KPIs are falling short.

There is a clear correlation between piloting an aircraft and piloting a business. The success of your leadership journey depends on you knowing what you need to measure to achieve your business goals and focusing on the right things at the right time. And don't forget to scan the external environment to keep an eye on what the competition is doing so you can measure your performance against theirs and set KPIs to stay ahead in your industry.

SWOT and PESTEL

In addition to KPIs, there are a couple of important analytical models that can give you very useful information about where time needs to be spent in your organisation. These tools are known as the SWOT and the PESTEL analysis.

SWOT is an acronym for:

- ➤ Strengths
- ➤ Weaknesses
- ➤ Opportunities
- ➤ Threats

The strengths and weaknesses relate to organisational analysis and the internal resources of the company. Where are your organisation's strengths and where are its weaknesses? The answers will give you an idea of where to introduce KPIs to play on your business strengths while mitigating your weaknesses.

The resources to analyse here will include:

- ➤ Human (your people)
- ➤ Financial (profit and loss, balance sheet and cash flow)
- ➤ Material (buildings, machines, furniture etc)

> Intangible (patents, copyright, rights of use etc)

The opportunities and threats come from the external environment. What's happening outside of your company? What is your competition doing?

The best way to analyse external factors is to use the PESTEL analysis. In fact, PESTEL is an acronym that represents the main external factors that are likely to impact your company or organisation:

> Political
> Economic
> Social
> Technological
> Environmental
> Legal

If we take three of the factors from this list – economic, social and environmental – we are talking about one of the most major considerations for all businesses today as these three are the foundations of Corporate Social Responsibility (CSR).[1]

A company has to be profitable and continue operating because it has a fiduciary responsibility to all of its stakeholders (the shareholders, employees, custodians and managers) while ensuring that it pays its taxes and respects all of the current regulations, thus participating in the wider social economy. A company's social responsibility is to do with how it treats its employees. It's also to do with its stance on diversity and inclusion, and on helping the local or wider community. The environmental part relates to whether or not a company is acting in a responsible and sustainable way. What, for example, is it doing about reducing its carbon footprint, increasing its use of renewable energy and recycling? Make sure your company or organisation has a CSR policy in place and takes it seriously.

Looking for external factors which may positively or negatively affect outcomes for your business is often known as environmental scanning. Famous examples are the United States subprime mortgage crisis, which led to the global financial crisis of 2008, and the impact of the lockdowns in 2020 and 2021 due to the Covid pandemic.

Of course, these would have been nigh on impossible to predict and legislate for, even with the most detailed of analysis. However, they are extreme examples; in the main, it's important to be aware of what is going on in the wider world that could affect your business, and use analytical models to your advantage to build an effective strategy and implement the correct KPIs to prevent firefighting to a large extent.

KPIs and analytical models help you to determine where to spend time in your business. However, they aren't the only considerations. Are you someone who believes in leading by example? Do you take control when there is a crisis situation and only give your people autonomy and empowerment when things are going well? In other words, are you adapting your style to different contexts and situations?

Your core beliefs concerning what being a good or great manager is all about will affect where you use your time. To consider this, there really is only one question to answer: where is all the analysis necessary to ensure that you reach the most positive outcomes in your organisation going to be done? In your office? Are you going to do everything yourself?

No?

I thought not.

This leads us nicely into our next chapter, which will discuss *who* you will be working with to ensure positive outcomes for you, your people and the business.

[1] Corporate Social Responsibility (NI Business Info)
https://www.nibusinessinfo.co.uk/content/what-corporate-social-responsibility

WHO

Time to Manage

An agenda for effective leadership

5WH

WHO

As a manager or leader, you will rarely be working on your own. As the 17th century English poet John Donne wrote:[1]

"No man is an island."

In other words, no man – or woman – can go through life completely isolated from their fellow human beings. And let's face it, your job is about managing complex tasks – which require several expert inputs – and leading people.

No matter how hard you try, you cannot become an expert in every single area of the business. This goes back to the SW of the SWOT model – if you're to be effective as a leader, acknowledge your own strengths and weaknesses as well as those of your people.

At times, you will need expert advice on areas crucial to your teams' success. There's no disgrace in admitting that someone on your team, or one of your teams, can do certain tasks far better than you can; in fact, a wise leader recognises their weaknesses as well as their strengths and surrounds themselves with experts who are better at these tasks than they are. There's also no disgrace in getting an expert in from outside if this will benefit you and your teams.

As a manager and leader, you need to be working and communicating with all of the following groups of people in the workplace:

> ➤ Your direct reports (often called the executive team)
> ➤ Middle management (often described as operational management)
> ➤ Supervisory employees (often described as hands-on management as they're directly supervising employees on the shop floor)
> ➤ Shop-floor employees (often known as line employees).

Whatever level of management you are at right now, the same rules of conduct and best practices apply. Although you will spread your time throughout the entire workforce, you will need to spend a lot of time with your direct reports on an individual or team basis. The most fundamental reason for this is alignment.

Alignment

We can look at alignment in two contexts when talking about leadership and management:

> ➤ Moral alignment
> ➤ Productive alignment

What do I mean by moral alignment? This is to do with ensuring that you and your team are all speaking the "same language" and promoting the core values and culture of the company. Importantly, you and all leaders in the company or organisation need to be seen to be doing so. This is to do with practising what you preach or, more pertinently, managing by example.

Let's imagine that among the core values of your company culture are:

- ➤ A safe working environment that promotes innovation where all of your people have their say within the context of a highly participative management style
- ➤ Integrity and honesty
- ➤ An HR policy designed and based on the precepts of:
  - o Internal promotion opportunities
  - o Succession planning
  - o The importance of training and development
  - o Learning from mistakes rather than individuals or teams being punished for them.

This sounds great, doesn't it? But what alignment really means is senior management (the executive team) not just "talking the talk", they're also "walking the walk". If the members of the executive team are not setting the example of behaviours they want to see cascade down through the organisation, there will be little chance that the culture they desire will be represented or promoted by the employees.

So moral alignment means that the behaviours of management and employees (at all levels) are in line with the stated values and beliefs of the organisation. What about productive alignment, though? How does it differ from moral alignment?

The clue is in the name. To be both efficient and effective, the goals and objectives of the organisation need to be in line with the core values. Moreover, productive alignment means that there needs to be shared goals and objectives throughout the organisation to ensure that there's not unnecessary friction between operating departments or operational and support functions.

If we are talking, for example, about total quality management and processes based on continuous improvement, this would apply to all parts of the organisation. It would entail promoting:

- ➤ The quality of the product or service that we provide to our customers
- ➤ The quality of service provided by support functions to operational functions (support functions being HR, finance, IT, sales and marketing, general management, and administration)

> ➤ The quality of service provided by management to our internal customers who are, by definition, our employees

This applies transversely across the organisation as well as at all levels. As leaders, we have to spend time with people at all levels in the business and not only with the executive team.

Middle management

Middle management is of particular importance. Let's imagine that the whole of the executive team is perfectly aligned both morally and from the productive goals-driven point of view.

By the way, this does not mean that every single person in the executive team is always in complete agreement with their colleagues. Cultural and personal diversity will create a multitude of different points of view, and these will all have to be taken into account to make sure that no one feels uncomfortable with any decisions that the team comes to on acceptable behaviour.

What I am talking about is the executives reaching a consensus on what is and is not acceptable behaviour, and then putting it into action for the greater good of the company, whether or not they are in total personal agreement with each other. In other words, they have to present a united front.

So where does middle management come in? It is extremely important for the executives to spend time with middle managers and listen to any feedback they have regarding alignment.

Let's imagine that operational goals and objectives are not cascading down properly to the middle management level. I'm sure you can guess what will happen by the time the operational objectives hit the shop floor: basically, a complete mess as no one will have any clarity on what they're supposed to achieve or how they're supposed to behave.

Clarity is one of the main reasons that leaders need to demonstrate as well as articulate the behaviours they have agreed are in the best interests of the organisation. This means, of course, spending time with people at all levels to ensure that there is alignment on core values, beliefs and objectives, but particularly with middle management. People at this level are, after all, best placed to communicate upwards, downwards and transversally. If we use the analogy of a motor vehicle, middle managers take the role of the transmission, which allows the car to understand what the engine needs to be doing at any given moment.

You as leader and your executive team also need to spend time with supervisors and line employees. The people at these levels not only need to know why they are doing things and behaving in a certain way, i.e. in line with the company values that you and the other executives are living and demonstrating through your own behaviours, they also need to feel respect and care from management at all levels.

This doesn't mean that you and the other executives don't trust middle management to communicate with their teams. A great way to demonstrate this trust is through delegation.

Let's say you have delegated a task, which needs to be done urgently, to middle management. For them to carry out the task correctly, you have to make sure several conditions are met:

> The manager must be competent enough to carry out the task
> They must be motivated to carry out this particular task
> They must know the exact scope of the task

Let's assume that you have covered all of the above points and correctly delegated the task (not just distributed it) to middle management. As leader, you have the right to check in with the manager to see how they are getting on with the task in question. Far from indicating a lack of trust in the ability of the middle manager to complete the task successfully, this is actually an important aspect of delegation as it allows them to explain how they are getting on, let you know whether or not they have sufficient resources and ask you for any help and advice they need.

Line employees

As a leader, you need to spend time with line employees because:

> ➢ It shows that you care about them as people
> ➢ It shows that you care about what they are doing in the company or organisation
> ➢ It allows you to check first hand if they have all of the necessary tools and training to be productive
> ➢ It allows you to check that communication is working well upwards, downwards and across the organisation
> ➢ It allows you to learn directly from the shop floor

The people who know most about how to get the job done are those who are actually doing it, so you as leader need to find time to listen to them. Otherwise, you will miss opportunities for improvement. By listening to your line employees, you can learn from the past, live in the present and plan for the future; a concept that is key to making sure you use your precious commodity, time, to your best advantage.

A line worker has already learned from their experience. Their main concern now will be getting the job done. However, as a manager, you're concerned about what lessons your teams have learned in the past and how you can use those lessons in planning for the future.

As an example, imagine that you're having a conversation with one of your people who, in the light of their hands-on experience, comes up with an idea which will be a total game changer for the product or service. You're the person who can plan for the future and make it happen while ensuring that the employee receives the credit for learning from the past and applying their learning in the present. It really would be a great shame if you hadn't taken the time to listen to your line workers on that particular day.

This brings us neatly to the end of Part One: 'The 5Ws'. We've asked what, why, when, where and who? Now we know *what* we need to be doing and *why* we need to be doing it, along with *when*, *where* and with *whom*, let's now see in Part Two *how* we are going to put all of this together. This will deliver a working model and framework which will help us understand exactly how to manage our own time and that of the organisation as a whole.

---

[1] Donne, J (1623) "Meditation XVII" (*Devotions upon Emergent Occasions*)
http://www.luminarium.org/sevenlit/donne/meditation17.php

PART TWO – THE 1H

HOW – SHORT- AND MEDIUM-TERM PLANNING

Time to Manage

An agenda for effective leadership

5WH

HOW – SHORT- AND MEDIUM-TERM PLANNING

It's likely that you have heard of the five Ps of planning: "proper planning prevents poor performance". You may also have heard the old Army version, the six Ps: "proper planning and preparation prevent piss-poor performance". However many Ps you want to consider, this brings us back to the wise words often attributed to Benjamin Franklin:

"If you fail to plan, you are planning to fail."

The truth of the matter is that hardly any of us (and I include myself in this) take time out of our busy schedules to do just that: plan. When we're caught up in the action, trying to do too many things at once or exhausted from getting things done as quickly as we can to meet impossible deadlines – along with the firefighting that inevitably comes hand in hand with this – it seems like a real step backwards to stop, look at what we are doing on a day-to-day basis and plan how to go about it more effectively.

Another phrase that many of us hear regularly is "Actions speak louder than words". As a result of this, we spend all our time doing and none or very little planning. However, there's an opposing point of view – one both my mother and my wife have been trying to teach me for many years: "More haste, less speed". In other words, if we rush into doing a task without thinking it through, it will likely throw up all kinds of problems that we haven't anticipated and take us longer to complete than if we'd made a proper plan in the first place. Alternatively, if we slow down initially and take the time to think and plan our strategy properly before acting, it will not only lead to better outcomes for all involved, but these outcomes will arrive in a much more timely manner.

As we delve into how to develop a framework for managing your precious time by working effectively, my first piece of advice to you is to STOP:

➢ **S**pend
➢ **T**ime
➢ **O**n
➢ **P**lanning

OK, so you've stopped whatever you were doing. What now?

Let's think how you are going to get yourself into the habit of planning. The first thing to do is to schedule time for it. This really is essential to using your time well.

An agenda for effective management means rather than doing things efficiently (which only comes with practice), choose to do the right things. One of my favourite quotes to underline this, usually attributed to Abraham Lincoln, is:

"Give me six hours to chop down a tree and I'll spend the first four sharpening the axe."

To become an effective leader, you need to concentrate on three types of planning:

- ➢ Short term
- ➢ Medium term
- ➢ Long term

In this chapter, we are going to look at the first two. Long-term planning will follow in the next chapter.

Short-term planning

On a daily basis, I strongly recommend that you maintain to-do lists. You can create your lists simply using a piece of paper or electronically if you prefer (there are plenty of applications available for this purpose).

The fact that you write a to-do list on a daily basis does not mean that you have to get everything on the list done that day. There are two reasons for this: a to-do list is dynamic and not everything on it will have the same level of priority.

This is the code I use for the items on my daily to-do list.

**	Something that has to be done today without fail, and it has to be done by me.
*	Something that at least has to be started on by me today, but is more of a medium- to long-term task.
A	Something that has to be started on today, but possibly by someone else.
B	Something that can wait for tomorrow, but no longer, and can be done by someone else.
C	Something that can be done in the near future, either by me or by someone else.

As I go forward, the dynamic nature of the list means items will gradually move up in priority from C to **.

However, you must ensure that you do not get caught up in the trap of what I call "to-doism". You do not have to plan every single thing that you have or want to do in a day. At its worst, to-doism could lead to unhealthy and even obsessive behaviour. Beware of this as it will cause stress rather than reducing it.

I recommend that you merge work and personal to-do items into one unique list. Why do I say that? Quite simply because your personal and work lives are intertwined.

Let's say, for example, that you don't take care of a medical problem in a timely manner because you haven't got around to booking an appointment with a doctor. Or maybe you forget your partner's birthday and don't book the weekend break that you promised them. The fallout from either example – an unpleasant atmosphere at home due to a hurt and angry partner, or a health issue that is getting progressively worse when it could so easily have been sorted out – will have a direct impact on your work as it will leave you in no condition to be an effective leader. As we discussed earlier, if you don't look after yourself, no one else is going to do it for you.

Let's now imagine that you are at the end of your work day. What you need to do at this point of the day is tick off all the tasks that you have done and transfer the not-done tasks to the next day's to-do list. And remember to give them new priority codes.

Then take your to-do list, put it out of sight and, more importantly, out of mind in a drawer (either in the office or at home) and *forget about it*. Do not come back to it until the following morning.

Let's say that you've finished today's list up to and including everything in category B. Remember to count this as a win and celebrate with a glass of your favourite wine, a meal in your favourite restaurant, a trip to the cinema, a workout – whatever you see as being a good way to reward yourself for a job well done. Not only will this make the process of short-term planning enjoyable, but it will positively reinforce the habit.

This whole process shouldn't take more than 10 minutes of your time in the morning and a further 10 minutes to update your to-do list in the evening. Take the time to save time. Remember the quote about sharpening the axe before chopping down a tree.

Now let's talk about medium-term planning.

Medium-term planning

This is something I do on a weekly basis, and I urge you to do so too. The way I approach this is to set time aside in my diary once a week to think or plan. In other words, I make appointments with myself. These appointments are set in stone unless, of course, an emergency occurs. And by emergency, I mean nothing less serious than the building being on fire.

What do I do with this thinking and planning time once a week? What am I recommending you do with your appointment with yourself? Use this time to reflect on what you have been doing, what you are currently doing and what you want to do in the future.

I'm sure that you have heard the expression "The writing was on the wall". This tends to be negative in nature, being said after something has gone (usually badly) wrong, but in this context, it is a positive thing to help you know exactly where you are with the objectives you or others have set for you.

How? I mean literally write your medium-term planning on the wall – or at least on a whiteboard. On my whiteboard, I list:

> ➢ KPIs to update
> ➢ Ongoing projects and progress reports to write
> ➢ Current priorities and issues to resolve

Like the daily to-do list, this is a dynamic system, allowing you to update KPIs and projects while thinking critically about your priorities and whether or not external or internal impacts have changed them.

This method also gives you the opportunity to take a step back and look at the big picture, avoiding confusion between what is urgent and what is important. But if you're still confused between urgent and important items on your to-do list, the Eisenhower matrix can help.[1] This is named after the 34th President of the United States who was also the Supreme Commander of the Allied Forces during the 2nd World War, so a man used to dealing with and differentiating between what is urgent and what is important.

Basically, you sort tasks on your to-do list into one of the four parts of the matrix. Let's take a look at each of the four parts of this matrix in conjunction with your to-do list.

Not urgent and not important: these are things to take off your short-term to-do list with immediate effect, or at least relegate them to Cs. Even looking at them is a waste of time as they will cause procrastination rather than anything else.

Urgent, but not important. Does something need to be done immediately, but it is probably not important enough to merit your undivided attention? In cases like these, delegate the task to another member of the team. These tasks equate to A and B on your to-do list.

Important and urgent. These tasks need to be taken care of with immediate effect and you need to do them personally, or at least be involved. They equate to the ** tasks on your daily to-do list.

Important, but not yet urgent. These tasks tend to be more to do with your long-term planning and your overall management and leadership strategy. They equate to the * tasks on your to-do list.

If you now go back to your whiteboard and draw an Eisenhower matrix on one side of it and updates to your KPIs on the other, you will be a in a good position to know where your priorities lie and how to manage your teams effectively.

In any system dealing with priorities, things can and often do change in terms of their urgency or importance. This is why we must get into the habit of updating our to-do lists on a daily and weekly basis to make sure that they are effective. Good habits make for good outcomes.

The 4Ds of time management[2] are inspired by and closely related to Eisenhower's matrix:

- ➢ **D**elete (not urgent, not important)
- ➢ **D**elegate (urgent, but not important)
- ➢ **D**o (important and urgent)
- ➢ **D**elay (important, but not urgent)

Whichever time-management tool you decide to use, have the discipline to stick with it. The saying "Plan your work, then work your plan" may be old, but it's still significant today. This basically means that to be effective, plans have to be translated into action at some point. Plans without action are nothing more than daydreams.

In this chapter, we have been talking about short- and medium-term planning. We have also been talking exclusively about how to plan our own time. Although this may make us effective both as people and as part of the organisation, it isn't sufficient to make us effective leaders.

In the next chapter, we will address this by talking about long-term planning.

[1] Introducing The Eisenhower Matrix (Eisenhower)
https://www.eisenhower.me/eisenhower-matrix/

[2] "The 4Ds of Time Management" (Product Plan)
https://www.productplan.com/glossary/4-ds-of-time-management/#:~:text=The%204%20Ds%20are%3A%20Do,what%20matters%20most%20to%20you.

HOW – LONG-TERM

PLANNING

Time to Manage

An agenda for effective leadership

5WH

HOW – LONG-TERM PLANNING

In the previous chapter, we looked at some tools and techniques that can keep us on track and effective with regard to how we use our time personally in the short to medium term. However, over the long term, we need to adopt a leadership style which will allow our teams to be both time efficient and effective.

To make sure this happens in the most painless way possible, I have created the Empowerment Triangle:

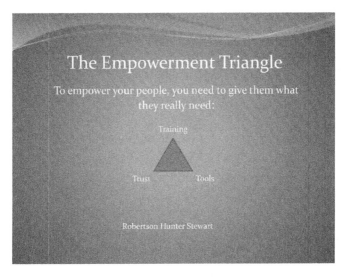

There are three major things we need to consider when looking at how to make our people effective:

training, providing the right tools and giving our people our trust. But before we go on to discuss each of these in more detail, let's first define what we mean by the word empowerment in this context.

Empowerment here means two things. Firstly, whatever the person's job is, they must feel empowered to carry it out on a daily basis without outside interference or help. For this to happen, they must have:

➢ A precise job description
➢ The knowledge of exactly how to do their job
➢ The autonomy to go so far in the decision-making process before asking for help
➢ The confidence to ask for help when they need it.

Secondly, they must feel empowered to express themselves. This means that:

➢ They must feel comfortable to do so without any fear whatsoever of reprisal
➢ They must have opportunities to do so.

Truly empowered employees will feel respected and trusted and will be working in a healthy and stress-free environment. Let's now discuss exactly how to get to this stage of empowerment for your teams by using each part of the triangle.

Training

I'm sure no organisation or company leader wants to spend money and time training people, only for them to leave. No, that's not ideal, but far worse is to have a workforce full of people who don't know what they're meant to be doing. This will inevitably lead to demotivation and possibly a toxic environment, with the result that people will leave anyway.

Far better to empower them by ensuring that you deliver the right kind of training in the right way and at the right time. I call this approach to training "from induction to the front line".

Obviously, this starts with the induction process itself. This helps new recruits to adjust and adapt to their surroundings and the company culture. You don't only want to introduce new employees to their colleagues, physical working environment and duties; you also want to give them information about the rules, regulations, traditions and core values that make up the company culture.

In management circles, there is often an onboarding process. This is where the new manager meets those they will be working with directly along with others in the organisation they will be expected to interact with. For frontline or shop-floor employees, it's a great idea to assign them a mentor during or immediately after the initial induction or onboarding process. This really helps people fit seamlessly in to the organisation with more ease and less stress.

Once the induction is done, you can look at job-specific training which will enable the employee to do the tasks outlined in their job description. The form this training takes will depend heavily on exactly what the job involves.

Certain jobs require theoretical or classroom training before the new recruit can carry out their tasks. For example, you would not expect a computer programmer to start coding before they have learned about the appropriate system or software. You would not expect a plumber or electrician to work on a building until they have had the appropriate industry-recognised training, for obvious safety reasons apart from anything else.

Other tasks require more hands-on or "on-the-job" training. Examples include waiting tables in a restaurant, serving drinks behind a bar or operating machinery on a production line or a cash till in a supermarket.

A lot of roles require a degree of academic education before the person even applies for a job. No one would want to put themselves in the hands of a doctor or dentist who'd had no formal education.

In summary, before being allowed to do a job, every new employee should be socially integrated into the company (through induction) and thoroughly trained so they are in possession of the adequate skills to perform the job that they are paid to do.

When a person is just starting out after induction and training, they will not be as efficient or effective as their more experienced counterparts. That brings us back to the idea of mentoring. When you assign an experienced mentor to a new member of your team, you are doing two things:

> ➢ Creating the conditions for the new employee to succeed, thus reducing the risk of unnecessary turnover
> ➢ Valorising the mentor by giving them responsibility and recognising their expertise

I'm a fan of mentoring and have used this often during my career with great overall results for the teams that I've worked with. Not only do people need to have the right training mix (theoretical and hands on), they also need to have the right amount of training compounded by mentoring until they are able to do their job with full autonomy. This may sound like it will cost your company or organisation a lot in terms of time, money and effort, but I can assure you that it's a lot less expensive than abnormal levels of staff turnover.

According to recent studies,[1] employee turnover for unskilled workers costs on average 50% of their annual salary, and the percentage only increases as you move up through skilled workers to middle and senior management and eventually to executives. At the very top of an organisation, the cost of replacement can be anywhere between 100 and 150% of annual salary. By comparison, the costs of onboarding and training your employees correctly are a lot less, and as a result they're more than justified.

Now we're clear on the importance of training, let's move on to talk about the second T of the Empowerment Triangle: providing the right tools.

Tools

To illustrate the importance of providing the right tools for your people to do their job, let's imagine some examples where this is not the case:

> ➢ A builder making cement without a spade
> ➢ A housekeeper cleaning a room without a vacuum cleaner
> ➢ A chef making a cake without flour or baking soda
> ➢ A joiner building a shed without a hammer
> ➢ A cashier having to enter product codes manually because the barcode scanner is broken – can you imagine the queues in the supermarket and the stress for the cashier?

These might all be extreme examples, but we don't have to get to these extremes before a lack of the right tools puts our people in stressful situations. They may even have the right tools, but not of a high enough quality.

Imagine, for example, that the joiner putting the shed together has a lightweight aluminium hammer. We are certainly going to be waiting a long time for that shed to be built! Imagine now that we give another joiner a heavyweight moulded-iron hammer. They will be able to build the shed a bit faster than their colleague with the inappropriately lightweight tool. Let's go absolutely mad and give a third joiner a nail gun. Now we're not only going to have our shed built in no time, it will probably be a lot more solid than it would have been otherwise.

When we provide the right tools and make sure they are good quality, our people can do their jobs quickly and well. They will also be far happier and less stressed than someone who doesn't have access to the right tools.

Providing the right tools and training can save our organisation enormous amounts of time, effort and money. And tools don't necessarily have to be physical in nature, particularly for people in management and leadership positions. Here, we could consider that preparation and training are the tools they require for the job. This is, unfortunately, where things tend to go wrong.

As an example, let's imagine that the managers in our organisation are not taught (or have not learned) the fundamentals of situational management. As a result, they probably won't know when a more directive type of management is required and when they need their style to be more participative, or when to coach someone and the stage in the individual's development process they can start to delegate to that person.

What about when managers are expected to evaluate the performance of their reports, but haven't actually been given any relevant or specific training on how to prepare for and carry out an appraisal interview? If we are ensuring that everyone else in the organisation has the adequate tools and training to carry out their job or task in the optimal way, why would we not do the same for our managers?

Examples of the types of training that would be useful for junior management include:

- ➢ Situational or contextual management
- ➢ Techniques and tools for better time management (for example the Eisenhower matrix or the 4Ds)
- ➢ Conflict management and how to deal with difficult conversations
- ➢ How to carry out an annual appraisal interview
- ➢ How to carry out a briefing in the optimal way
- ➢ How to organise and run effective meetings
- ➢ How to run one-to-one meetings with direct reports on a frequent basis.

If we don't give relevant and adequate training to our existing or prospective managers, we cannot expect them to be effective. Just because someone is excellent in their current role or expert in a particular area in the business, it doesn't mean that they will automatically make a good manager. Although internal promotion is in general a good thing, it can lead to the situation where we are setting people up to fail if we don't provide the correct leadership training.

It would seem obvious that the main competence a manager requires is the capacity to lead effectively. If you believe as I do that leading by example is fundamental, you'll be able to imagine the impact on the workforce if they realise that their managers are not "fit" to lead and have no real clue what they are doing, or even how to start going about it. This rapidly creates a situation where managers are no longer able to lead due to a complete lack of credibility.

Now that we recognise the importance of the correct training and tools, and where the training *is* the tool the employee requires to do their job properly, let's imagine that all of our management and leadership teams have been trained correctly and have all the tools that they need. How do they prioritise things so that they can practise people-centred and participative management and create the conditions where a culture of mutual confidence and trust can be born?

Trust

The fact that you have given sufficient training and resources to your teams (including your management team) is in and of itself a good foundation for gaining your people's trust. However, to reinforce this culture of trust further, you must take one basic thing into account and that is to be people rather than task focused. After all, the huge majority of tasks are carried out in the workplace by your people, not by you.

To gain the trust of an individual or your team, you need first and foremost to spend sufficient time with them and spend it in the right way. This, of course, means absolutely no micro-managing; instead, it means truly listening to their concerns, showing that you have understood them and acted upon them where necessary, and then making sure they know you're available to them if they need you, but leaving them to get on with the task in their own way.

Of course, if they don't deliver, you will have to intervene. However, once you've supplied the correct training and tools, you are likely to find the trust you can place in your people as a result will reap the ultimate reward: it will free up that most precious of commodities, time.

Now you know the importance to your people, especially those managing your teams, of the Triangle of Empowerment – training, tools and trust – it's time to look at an area that can be the greatest motivator of all. Only if it's handled correctly, though.

Yes, I'm talking about goals.

---

[1] Smith, G (17 September 2021) "Employee Retention: The real cost of losing an employee" (People Keep) https://www.peoplekeep.com/blog/employee-retention-the-real-cost-of-losing-an-employee

HOW – GOALS

Time to Manage

An agenda for effective leadership

5WH

HOW – GOALS

In this chapter, we are going to have a look at goal setting. This is an area where we as leaders need to have a high level of skill to be effective.

So, how exactly do we make sure we can not only set goals effectively, but manage our own and our teams' time optimally to ensure everyone is seeing their goals through to a successful conclusion? We need to:

> ➢ Ensure that the goals we give to individual team members are SMARTER
> ➢ Ensure that there are common goals for the team as a whole (creating alignment)
> ➢ Hold regular one-to-one meetings with all of our direct reports
> ➢ Hold effective team meetings on a regular basis
> ➢ Very importantly, maintain a participative style of management overall.

Let's now have a look at the first four points in more detail. We'll then cover the crucial fifth point, participative management, in the next chapter.

SMARTER goals

I'm sure you've heard of SMART objectives and goals. The acronym generally stands for goals being:

> ➢ Specific

- ➢ Measurable
- ➢ Attainable
- ➢ Relevant
- ➢ Timed

However, the theme can be adapted to whatever is relevant for your company or organisation. The acronym can also be extended, as you can see from the heading of this section: SMARTER goals.

What are SMARTER goals and objectives? Let's start by looking at what I mean by the acronym SMART:

- ➢ **S**pecific, **s**imple and with a highly defined **s**cope
- ➢ **M**easurable and **m**anaged
- ➢ **A**chievable but **a**mbitious, **a**greed upon by the whole team
- ➢ **R**elevant
- ➢ **T**imed and aligned with **t**eam objectives

To make SMART into SMARTER, I add that goals need to be:

- ➢ **E**mpowering

And include:

- ➢ **R**esults and **r**ecognition

Let's go back to the start of the SMARTER acronym and take a closer look at the S. By **s**imple, I don't mean that the objective is easy to achieve; I mean that it is both precise and concise. In other words, I can explain it clearly in writing and my teams can understand it with no difficulty, particularly the person who is going to be carrying out the work.

For scope, I either use the example of building a house that we looked at in the Introduction or a similar example relating to the task of renovating a hotel. Imagine you are in charge of this renovation, but you have no further information. Would you and your team have any idea where to start with this?

To define the scope of this project, you would need to ask a number of questions, including:

> Will my team and I only be renovating the bedrooms?
> Are we renovating all of the bedrooms?
> Are we only renovating the rooms on specific floors?
> Will we be renovating the restaurant and the bar?
> Will we be renovating the public areas?
> Will the hotel be fully or partially closed during the renovation?
> What kind of renovation are we talking about – changing everything in the rooms, or only the soft furnishings and furniture?

The point is, whatever the project you're involved in, you need a specific but simple outline of the scope to have any chance of success.

Next, let's take a look at M, specifically **m**easurable. There must be a way to measure whether or not the goal or objective has been achieved (in other words, you're not leaving things to chance). Otherwise, it will be difficult to **m**anage.

However, manage isn't just about measurement; it's also about how you manage objectives with your direct reports. What kind of checking or marker system will you have in place to track the objectives on a frequent basis throughout the year?

In most versions of SMART, the A only means **a**chievable. Obviously, this is extremely important; if you give people goals which are impossible to achieve, it will demotivate them rather than encourage them. Your people must have at least a chance of achieving the goals you set.

That said, the objective doesn't have to be easy to achieve, otherwise this too could demotivate your people. If you constantly give easy objectives to high achievers in your team, you're likely to find yourself in a situation where they become disinterested in what they are doing and, in some cases, decide to seek a more appropriate challenge elsewhere. So, your objectives for your team members must be **a**mbitious.

You don't just want to give goals and objectives willy-nilly to people and expect them to achieve them. The final A is **a**greement: you have to ensure that the team member agrees that the objective is part of their priorities and within their range of possibilities.

Now let's move on to R. **R**elevant here means two things. First of all, the goal or objective must have relevance to the work that the person you're giving it to is doing. You wouldn't ask a plumber to rewire the electrics in your house (the consequences could be catastrophic). Secondly, the goal or objective must be relevant to the team member's department and the organisation as a whole.

Timed is straightforward enough in the sense that each goal or objective has a due date for completion and the individual or team has a realistic amount of time to achieve it. Alignment with the objectives of the **t**eams across the organisation is extremely important. If you ask the production-line manager to increase product-manufacture output by 10% and at the same time ask the quality department for a 10% increase in the standards and conformity of the end product, you may have given objectives to these teams which are diametrically opposed. Would it not be better to assign the same objective to both teams and base it on output *and* quality? This would ensure that both teams work together to achieve their common objectives

What about **e**mpowering? What has that got to do with setting goals and objectives?

Everything, is the simple answer to this question. Firstly, as we saw in the previous chapter, empowerment is about ensuring that your teams have the right tools and training to do their jobs and meet their objectives in the most autonomous way possible. This means, for example, that in customer-facing environments, team members don't always have to ask their supervisor or manager for permission to make decisions; to a clearly defined extent, they are allowed to decide for themselves what's necessary to satisfy customers' needs and demands.

Let's take the example of giving a refund on a product that is not up to standard. The employee should know explicitly the level of refund they can give and be trained on how to go about this without outside help. Only when the refund goes over the limit will the team member need to ask for managerial assistance.

Empowerment does two things:

- ➢ It allows employees to take decisions and feel comfortable in doing so
- ➢ It reinforces the idea that the management team has confidence and trust in the employees' capability to do their job on a day-to-day basis

Last but by no means least, results and recognition. These are fundamental to the setting and achieving of goals and objectives. At some stage, you as a leader will need to judge whether or not your teams have achieved the goal or objective you set them.

Most organisational leaders address results and recognition during the end-of-year appraisal or evaluation interview. I would recommend, however, that this should take place on a much more regular basis. It is extremely important here to note that there are degrees of success you can recognise; it's not as simple as a pass or fail for each objective. You can also put in place a weighting system to give more or less importance to certain objectives compared to others.

Remember to link recognition and rewards to the overall level of success the individual or team has achieved. Much of the time, this reward can be in the form of a monetary bonus system, but it can also be related to promotion, succession planning, certain types of gifts (anything from a shopping voucher to a visit to Disneyland) or finally qualifying for a company car.

Whatever form the reward or recognition takes, it is important to recognise your employees' successes in some way. It's human nature for them to ask when set a goal or objective, "What's in it for me?" Make sure you can answer this question succinctly with a clear process of reward and recognition.

Common goals for the team

What are we talking about here? Common goals are the overall goals of the team as an entity, which also apply to all team members individually.

Overall goals for a team or organisation can be raising the level of employee or customer satisfaction, the market share or financial performance of the company. A goal may, for example, relate to the level of customer satisfaction obtained for the entire organisation.

When the reward and recognition aspect of goal setting is related to financial bonus systems, there's often a "financial gatekeeper" on the team. The reason for this is simple: for each individual to achieve the maximum potential for the bonus, the team's overall performance will need to be taken into account as well. There may also be non-financial gatekeepers if the team goal is reaching a certain percentage score for the internal branding audit or a global customer satisfaction score for the organisation as a whole.

Whatever goals you set for your organisation or team, it is important for everyone to understand that to maximise their own individual potential for reward and recognition, the team, department or organisation as a whole has to reach its common goals. This relates back to our discussion in the

"Who?" chapter regarding moral and productive alignment.

How do you go about ensuring that common goals are working? How do you put in place markers that allow you to see whether or not they are continuing to work over time? As a leader, you must keep your finger on the pulse and the best way to do this is by having frequent formal one-to-one meetings with each of your team members.

One-to-one meetings

These meetings are truly fundamental in ensuring that we use our time as managers in the most effective and efficient way possible. For one thing, regular one-to-ones avoid us wasting too much time firefighting against unforeseen events and dealing with unnecessary interruptions.

One-to-one meetings (sometimes called quality time) with our direct reports need to take place at least once a month and last for anywhere between one and two hours. Believe me, the short-term sacrifice of time pays huge dividends in terms of getting rid of those endless "Can I just have a quick word, boss?" requests that repeatedly keep us from the things we really want and need to be doing.

As a bare minimum, in a one-to-one, discuss the team member's goals and objectives and what kind of progress they're making towards achieving them, or not. Do they require supplementary resources and/or help at this particular time?

If they manage a team themselves, you also need to be discussing HR issues related to that team. This discussion can take the form of anything from offering advice on how to manage difficult conversations with one of their team members to the training, succession planning and ambiance of the team as a whole.

What's really important here is that you as leader take the role of coach during these meetings. Listen a lot more than you speak, which gives your team member room to express themselves and feel comfortable in proposing new or innovative ideas.

Another important aspect of these meetings is that they need to be structured with recurring themes such as HR, objectives, operations and financials. In addition to these structured sections, make time to have an informal chat about how the team member is feeling concerning their work and life in general.

A golden rule of one-to-one meetings is that under no circumstances whatsoever should they be interrupted – unless, of course, the building is burning down. Don't forget, this is quality time you are spending with the individual in question and you must both see it as such. Never answer your phone or write an SMS in the middle of the meeting.

An interesting point about one-to-one meetings is to do with ownership – you give a high degree of ownership for the meeting to your employee. How do you go about this? In the main, by doing two things.

First, it is the employee who takes and writes up the minutes for the meeting and sends them to you before their next one-to-one. Secondly, apart from the recurring themes, it is the team member who sets the agenda and suggests additional items for discussion. This idea goes hand in hand with the autonomy and empowerment you want all your team members to feel.

One-to-one meetings allow you to make plans with the individuals in your team and set a marker against each one which shows where the team members are in relation to the objectives you both set at the beginning of the year. They also allow you to carry out contingency planning to take into account external conditions (for example an economic downturn or a pandemic) which make it impossible to reach these goals or objectives. Then you can reset the priorities with your people.

Last but by no means least, one-to-one meetings allow you to build long-lasting relationships with your people based on mutual confidence and trust.

Team meetings

People often talk about meeting mania or complain about what a waste of time team meetings are. They always have "better" things to do than attend the meeting.

We've all probably been in a meeting at one time or another that has made us wonder what the heck we're doing there. If that resonates with you, it's likely to be because you really *shouldn't* have been in that meeting in the first place. This type of meeting is like the email which everyone in the entire organisation is copied in to "just in case". This often happens in toxic work environments because people are either protecting themselves from unwanted comeback or trying to win points over their teammates.

Make sure that you always invite the right people to your meetings, particularly when they are meetings which are transversal in nature. For team meetings, it's quite clear who to invite: the members of the relevant team, or at least enough representatives to make sure everyone on the team has a say and knows what the outcome is.

So, now you know who to invite, how do you run the meeting properly? Here are some guidelines you may find helpful:

- ➤ Always define what the meeting is about in advance, including the scope and who exactly needs to be present
- ➤ Set out the amount of time the meeting will take. Remember, your people also have schedules and to-do lists, so name a timekeeper for each meeting
- ➤ Send out a written agenda for the meeting a few days in advance (i.e., not the night before the meeting) and ensure that everyone invited receives a copy
- ➤ Appoint someone to take and write up minutes of each meeting using a consistent structure. For example:
  - o People present
  - o Date
  - o Information to be shared:
    - ▪ Subject 1
    - ▪ Subject 2
  - o Round table
  - o Work in progress and due dates.

So, you need someone to chair the meeting, a timekeeper and someone to take minutes. As the manager, you will normally be chair and ensure that the meeting is as participative as possible while exercising a certain amount of control so the attendees stick to the agenda, people are not interrupted and things go smoothly. You will also be in charge of setting the agenda, although team members can, of course, suggest and contribute subjects too (and it's healthy to ensure that this happens as much as possible).

I usually start team meetings off by going through the minutes from the last meeting to look at the progress the team has made since in regard to operational goals that we set, work in progress, and due and completion dates. I then move forward to updates and information regarding the company, the team and what's new in the organisation. The main subjects for discussion on the agenda come next, after which I suggest a round table where each person has the opportunity to share information regarding their particular service, department or area of interest. This format has always worked well for me and my teams.

There are two crucial aspects to ensuring an empowering culture around team meetings. Firstly, all team meetings in an organisation or company need to be run in the same way – the most highly participative manner possible. Secondly, hold meetings with the same frequency for all departments and services below executive level within the organisation. I usually recommend once a month for most teams, with the executive team meeting at least once a week.

Why is it so important that all teams meet with the same frequency? Again, this is about alignment. It ensures that employees know that they are all treated fairly and what they have to say is given equal importance wherever they sit in the organisation. It also ensures that communication and information flow correctly within the organisation, whether it is vertically or horizontally.

For information to flow properly up and down the organisation and across departments with as little interference as possible, you require a certain number of processes. These ensure that everyone is working with the best quality of information. This quality information is extremely important as it reduces the risk of rumours spreading unnecessarily, and rumours often lead to toxicity.

Open, honest and regular discussion at all levels is the best way to fight toxicity in your company or organisation. SMARTER goals, alignment between team objectives and the overall goals of the organisation, and a culture of one-to-one and team meetings are all crucial to make sure communication channels always remain open.

This leads us nicely on to the next chapter where we will be discussing the all-important participative-management style.

HOW – PARTICIPATIVE

MANAGEMENT

Time to Manage

An agenda for effective leadership

5WH

HOW – PARTICIPATIVE MANAGEMENT

In the 1970s, Paul Hersey and Kenneth Blanchard first developed what they called the "Lifecycle Theory of Leadership".[1] They then decided to rename and update the model to "Situational Leadership".[2] Finally, in the late 70s and early 80s, Blanchard and his colleagues developed the Situational Leadership 2 model.[3]

The Situational Leadership model, as the name suggests, brings to light that there is no one style of leadership or management that fits all situations. However, the model underlines that we are not just referring to situations and context; we are also referring to different ways to manage depending on who we are talking to and, more specifically, their level of competence and/or motivation.

The model explains that there are four main types of management: directive, negotiated, participative and delegative. I personally believe that the most effective method of managing both individuals and teams always comes through maximum participation, as shown in my model on the next page:

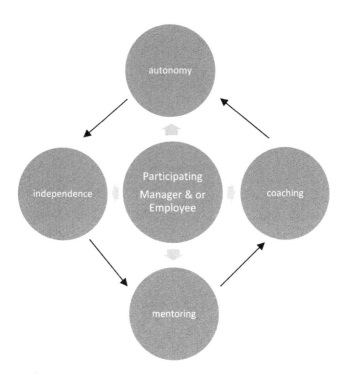

This model is both linear and dynamic for the individual and the organisation. For an individual, the stages of development go from the need to be mentored, to coached, to autonomy and finally independence over time and with experience. However, the same individual can find themselves at different places in the cycle for different subjects, circumstances or contexts.

Whether it is the manager or the employee who is in the centre, there is always participation in the development of an individual or team from both sides (management and employee). When mentoring rather than coaching is required for a team member, for example, the team member has to participate to ensure that they are learning properly. In a coaching mode, the manager will be asking more questions concerning what the team member thinks about their own performance and allowing more room for them to find their own solutions rather than being told what to do, as they would be in the case of mentoring.

When the team member has more autonomy, the manager needs to hold discussions with them regarding potential solutions to specific problems or areas for further improvement. At the stage of independence, the employee has a high degree of autonomy and the leader will ensure that this "degree" is well defined so that the employee knows when they need or want to hold discussions with the leader or their line manager (for example, during their one-to-one meeting).

This is a highly dynamic people model as it depends on what the manager and team member are talking about (the same person can find themselves at different places on the model depending on the subject). It also depends on time (people can find themselves participating in different ways at different times).

The most important thing in the participative management model is that people (both managers and employees) are interacting to their maximum potential. The manager's role here is to constantly encourage their people to co-participate in their own development, the generation of ideas and solutions, and the realisation of individual, team and company goals (alignment).

Whatever the situation or the stage of development a team member may be at, we are always talking about participation from all involved, albeit in different types and degrees. This is related to holding one-to-one meetings regularly. And it applies not only to individuals, but to the team as a whole.

The advantages of participation

As the old saying goes, "Two heads are better than one".[4] The more that we and our people are involved in discussions, the more likely we are to find a rapid solution to a given problem.

Collective intelligence, particularly the positive impact this can have on the company in terms of the levels and speed of creativity and innovation, is yet another example of using your and your people's time effectively. After all, problem solving using collective intelligence (group coaching and brainstorming, for example) will yield ideas and potential solutions much faster than trying to do things on your own.

There is another aspect to participative management which reinforces it as a great time saver. Because you and your people are finding solutions together, they will be much easier to put in place due to the fact that you will already have a consensus among your teams regarding how to move forward.

This is not always the case with a top-down method of management. Using this style of management, you as leader may make decisions faster than you would with the participative mode, but you are also far more likely to come up against resistance from your people. This is purely due to the fact that you didn't consult them on the way to making the decision, so they don't feel invested in it in any way. If they have been involved in the decision – for example, finding a solution to a problem or developing a strategy – they are much more likely to act on it.

To summarise, participative management is more time effective than the leader working alone because of:

- ➤ Collective intelligence allowing better solutions to be found within a shorter time frame
- ➤ Faster translation from vision and/or ideas to action due to general consensus regarding solutions
- ➤ Accelerated development and better and quicker acquisition of competence
- ➤ The construction of relationships based on mutual confidence and trust.

Overall, a participative management style or method allows you to put pressure on time itself instead of creating time pressure for your people.

The last bullet point is one of the most important recurring themes in this book. The relationship between trust and political behaviour is inversely proportional, and too much in the way of politics lessens the effectiveness of any organisation or company.

TRUST to build trust

So, what does trust actually look like? The acronym TRUST sums it up perfectly:

- ➢ **T**ruth
- ➢ **R**ecognition
- ➢ **U**nderstanding
- ➢ **S**upport
- ➢ **T**ime

Telling the truth may seem an obvious aspect of trust, and it is. However, the *way* that we tell people the truth is important. As a manager or leader, we need to choose the words we use extremely carefully.

For example, instead of telling someone that they are no good at something, it's better to tell them that there is still room for improvement. When someone does something exceptionally well, we tell them not only that they've done a great job, but exactly why what they've achieved is so important. This reinforces purpose.

The best way to understand the fundamental importance of telling the truth is to imagine telling a lie or lying by omission, and then being found out by your people. You may have spent weeks, months or even years building trust with your people, but the instant they discover you have lied to them, that trust is lost for good.

Recognition builds trust. First and foremost, make sure you remember each team member's name and some key facts about them. When is their birthday? Are they married or single? Do they have children? Do they prefer rugby or football? What are their hobbies?

Of course, it would be impossible to remember details about everyone in a huge organisation, but it's essential you know the team members you interact with on a regular basis as human beings as well as work colleagues. It's not just about remembering their name and their role in your team, but also who they are. We all like to be remembered for *who* we are and not just for what we do.

Recognition, of course, goes further than that; it's also to do with congratulating and rewarding people for a job well done. This is part and parcel of positive reinforcement, encouraging people in the team to repeat desired behaviours and outcomes.

Understanding is extremely important, particularly with regard to the effectiveness of your communication with each team member. There are two parts to this.

The first is showing understanding through your verbal and non-verbal communication when you are having a discussion, for example by reformulating what someone has just said to you in your own words and checking you have understood. Secondly, there is showing empathy when a team member is facing a difficult situation. You do not have to solve all of their personal issues, but you do have to show that you care about them if you want your colleagues to care about you and your opinion.

This is called reciprocity. It underlines the fact that as a leader, you recognise that you have to give your support freely to your people in the first instance to earn their trust over the long term.

Support takes many forms. It can be giving someone time off to resolve a personal issue, for example, but it is about a lot more than moral support. It's about giving your support to team members' ideas, opinions, projects, ambitions and objectives.

Finally, when building TRUST, we come back to the overarching theme of the book: time. Without giving your people adequate amounts of your time through well-designed meetings (either individual or team), you will not be in any position to gain their trust. In any relationship, whether personal or professional, trust builds over time.

Sharing quality time with your people is crucial if you wish to build sustainable relationships with and between them. As I'm fond of saying:

"You've got to make the time if you want to save the time."

And these words bring Part Two, the "How?" of 5WH, rather neatly to a conclusion.

[1] Hersey, P; Blanchard, KH (1969) "Lifecycle Theory of Leadership" (*Training and Development Journal*, 23, 5, pp26–34)

[2] Hersey, P; Blanchard, KH (1977) *Management of Organizational Behaviour: Utilizing human resources* (Prentice Hall)

[3] Blanchard, KH; Zigarmi, P; Zigarmi, D (1985) *Leadership and the One-minute Manager: Increasing effectiveness through situational leadership* (Marrow)

[4] Speake, J (2015) *Oxford Dictionary of Proverbs* (Sixth edition, Oxford University Press)

CONCLUSION

Time to manage

An agenda for effective leadership

5WH

CONCLUSION

Let's return to the key message of this book – making the most of your valuable commodity, time. To do this effectively, you need to STOP:

- ➢ **S**pend
- ➢ **T**ime
- ➢ **O**n
- ➢ **P**lanning

Always make sure that you have the time to step back from what you are doing. STOP and take a look at the big picture, and give yourself adequate time to do this properly.

You may be familiar with the expression mentioned earlier: "More haste, less speed". Basically, if you do things too quickly, you will end up losing much more time on firefighting and resolving issues in the long run than you would have done if you had planned and prepared properly.

In management and leadership, it's a marathon, not a sprint. If you try to sustain a sprint over a long distance, you are not going to make it very far. Remember that self-care is essential to your ability to manage both your time and your people effectively. You cannot and will not lead effectively if you are sprinting for the finish line and leaving yourself in no condition to plan properly, communicate well and build those all-important relationships along the way. You need to make the right choices as a manager and leader concerning how to use your time optimally.

People-focused management is not about doing things right (i.e. efficiently); it's much more to do with using your time to do the right things (i.e. effectively). However, efficiency is important, in particular with regard to the tools and/or systems you need to manage your time effectively. In other words, you need to be efficient at using these tools to be or become effective. My advice here is to choose the tool(s) and/or system(s) that suits you best and stick with it until using it becomes a habit.

At the beginning of the book, we talked about the triangle of fire. A fire can't start unless you have three main ingredients: fuel, oxygen and heat. If one of the elements is missing, the fire won't light, let alone burn. The comparison with the Empowerment Triangle we met in the "Long-term Planning" chapter is obvious in the sense that if any of the triangle's elements are missing, true empowerment cannot and will not take place.

Trust is the oxygen that allows employees to reach their maximum potential, provided they have the right **tools** (fuel) and are **trained** (ignited) to use them in the right way. But there is one thing missing from the Empowerment Triangle in the "Long-term Planning" chapter and that is time itself. In the simplest terms, you have to use your time properly to avoid time leaks.

On the next page is a more complete adaptation of the Empowerment Triangle.

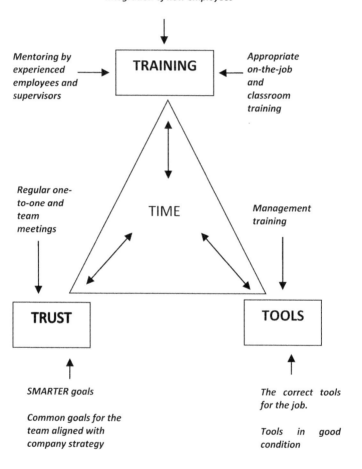

Good onboarding and
integration of new employees

Mentoring by
experienced
employees and
supervisors

TRAINING

Appropriate
on-the-job
and
classroom
training

Regular one-
to-one and
team
meetings

TIME

Management
training

TRUST

TOOLS

SMARTER goals

Common goals for the
team aligned with
company strategy

The correct tools
for the job.

Tools in good
condition

Each of the three main points of the triangle – trust, training and tools – now shows what you need to ensure the optimum conditions for the effective use of time.

Training:

> ➤ Good onboarding and integration process for new employees
> ➤ Appropriate and well-timed on-the-job and classroom training
> ➤ Mentoring by experienced employees and/or supervisors until the employee has sufficient autonomy

Tools:

> ➤ Management and/or leadership training. Without adequate soft-skills training, managers do not have the necessary tools to do their job effectively
> ➤ All the correct tools each and every employee needs for the job
> ➤ The tools must be in good condition and functioning correctly

Trust:

> ➤ SMARTER goals for team members and common goals for the team as a whole properly aligned with the company strategy

- ➢ Regular one-to-one and team meetings carried out at a consistent and appropriate frequency and in the proper way
- ➢ A highly participative style of management throughout all stages of an employee's development

If you put the details of the triangle into action in the ways described in this book, you will be creating the optimal conditions for the free flow of information within your organisation. This leads to people at all levels feeling able to communicate effectively in a safe environment. By safe, I am talking about both physically and psychologically. As manager and leader, always remember you are responsible for the wellbeing of your teams and team members.

Before I bring the book to a close, I would like to share one final acronym to sum up what is truly fundamental for us all as managers and leaders – TIME itself:

- ➢ **T**rain
- ➢ **I**nspire
- ➢ **M**anage
- ➢ **E**mpower

Training is, of course, one of the cornerstones of the Empowerment Triangle. To put this in context, think about a time in your past when you weren't properly trained and were instead thrown in at the deep end. Many of us – I include myself here – will have had an experience of this kind at one time or another. In a work setting, lack of proper training always leads to disengaged employees, which in turn leads to higher-than-expected turnover and extra recruiting and training costs. I am constantly amazed at the number of company and organisational leaders who don't seem to understand this.

When there is an economic downturn in the wider world, the training budget is often one of the first things to fall victim in an organisation. However, a key success factor in our fast-changing world and work environment is adaptability. Without a properly trained workforce, an organisation will not be ready for the upturn in the economy when it arrives as it won't be able to adapt to new internal or external conditions. It will then lose competitive advantage as it won't have sufficient agility to change direction or innovate.

Proper training, along with adapting this training to changing needs and contexts, promotes a healthy working environment where employees can thrive and prosper together with the organisation as a whole. A real win-win situation for all concerned.

What do I mean by inspire? Here, I am talking about extrinsic forms of motivation which inspire people to find their purpose and place within the organisation. It's inspirational motivation that brings about a sense of belonging through the potential to earn rewards and recognition related to excellence in performance, for example up-selling or repeat sales. This kind of motivation includes bonus systems, and can go as far as profit sharing where the employee has a real financial stake in the continued success of the company.

Although financial reward is important, it is by no means the only form of motivation to inspire people to excellence. One of the easiest and most effective ways to inspire people to do the things and exhibit the behaviours you want is by listening to them.

When you are truly listening to someone, perhaps during a well-run one-to-one, you are inspiring them to share information and ideas with you. When they see some of their ideas translated into concrete action and receive proper recognition for this, that team member will feel inspired to share even more insights in the future.

The word "manage" brings us back to the basics of managing our own time and that of our people correctly. As leaders, we are there to inspire and influence our people towards action, but there are things we need to manage to do this. Most of them involve self-management – to manage our time and our people effectively, we must be sure to look after ourselves.

By using the tools and techniques we have discussed in this book effectively, you are taking the time to make time. Because you are planning your and your teams' time, you will have the time to deal with any situations which might arise. When you and your teams learn from the past, live for today and plan for tomorrow, you are all involved in almost continual contingency planning through individual and team communication.

The word "empower", of course, relates back to the Empowerment Triangle. The only point to add on this subject is the importance of bringing your people from onboarding to autonomy and empowerment as quickly as possible.

Doing this without sacrificing quality presupposes that you have standard operating procedures in place regarding induction and onboarding, and deliver job-specific training as and when people arrive in the company. In other words, you have planned and prepared for each new employee's arrival in advance.

Planning that leads to appropriate decision making and action, along with training, empowerment, adaptability and trust, will always be the foundation upon which organisations develop a long-term future for their stakeholders. As we move into that future, the true strength of leadership will be recognised as caring for our people while building on this foundation.

We need to empower our people by training them appropriately, and then trust in their capacity to do their job without direct supervision or unnecessary interference. This will bear fruit in the form of them trusting us enough to give their invaluable insights into how the organisation can move forward, ensuring a continual culture of innovation and adaptability.

The 5WH structure allows us to answer the most pertinent questions regarding the optimum use of our own and our people's time. More than that, these questions are fundamental to understanding and solving complex organisational problems. In fact, they are at the very core of problem solving throughout our lives.

By adopting the management techniques and principles we've talked about in this book, you will be in a position to manage your time and create your own unique and effective agenda for leadership.

Printed in Great Britain
by Amazon

13191241R00108